for Louise £2-40

C000085766

Christina & Stephen.

THE
WHOLESOME
FOOD
COOKBOOK

THE
WHOLESOME
FOOD
COOKBOOK

MAGGIE BLACK

DAVID & CHARLES
Newton Abbot   London   North Pomfret (Vt)

For Ewart Wells

British Library Cataloguing in Publication Data

Black, Maggie
  The wholesome food cookbook.
  1. Cookery
  I. Title
  641.5   TX717

  ISBN 0-7153-8229-2

Typeset by ABM Typographics Limited, Hull
and printed in Great Britain
by Redwood Burn Limited, Trowbridge, Wilts
for David & Charles (Publishers) Limited
Brunel House   Newton Abbot   Devon

Published in the United States of America
by David & Charles Inc
North Pomfret   Vermont 05053   USA

CONTENTS

◆◆

	Weights and Measures	6
	Introduction	7
1	Good Products to Use	9
2	Meat and Fish: Making the Most of Them	15
3	Good Value: Poultry and Small Game	40
4	Dairy Foods to Best Advantage	63
5	Making Your Own Breads	78
6	Spreads for Your Bread	100
7	Vegetables in Plenty	115
8	Good Value Herb Products	142
9	Making the Most of Fruit	156
10	Extra Flavour to Your Food	175
11	Good Value Treats	192
	Books to Read	196
	Acknowledgements	197
	Index	198

WEIGHTS AND MEASURES

—◆◇◆—

The ingredients in the recipes are measured first in English ounces, pounds, pints or fluid ounces, and spoonfuls; then, after '/' in grams and kilograms, millilitres and litres; and thirdly, in brackets after the ingredient's name, in American cups or spoons when English measures are inconvenient or give different quantities. British Standard metric measures have been used throughout, based on the 25-gram unit. American measures follow those laid down by the US Bureau of Standards. All cups are light to medium packed unless otherwise stated.

All spoons should be measured level; they should be filled slightly above the rim of the spoon, then levelled off with a knife blade. To save space, metric equivalents are not given for spoonfuls, and they are abbreviated to tbsp and tsp.

Australians, South Africans and Canadians who want to cook from this book should remember that the American cup holds 8fl oz (200ml) and the standard tablespoon holds approximately 15ml, whereas the measuring cups or spoons they use at home may hold different quantities.

Either the English *or* the metric measures will give a good product, but one or the other must be used for measuring all the ingredients in a particular recipe; they must not be mixed. Americans, however, can use their own measures (given in brackets) instead of some of the British measures in any particular recipe.

INTRODUCTION

—◆◇◆—

The idea of writing this book came from reading about cooks in the past, especially Victorian cooks from about 1850 onwards — not the chefs of the wealthy but workaday family cooks! Having hitherto used virtually nothing but natural, local foodstuffs, the cooks of middle-class Victorians in particular found themselves faced, from then on, with a growing number of new processed or 'convenience' foods made in an anonymous distant factory or brought in bulk from overseas.

Some of the new foods, such as jams, were mass-production cheap goods. Others appealed as novelties to the affluent. Neither type, on the whole, made meals as nourishing or palatable as fresh, untainted foodstuffs but they were certainly convenient, for instance roller-milled flour, dried packeted soups, custard powder and canned meats! An honest cook, if she could afford to choose, had to decide which of the new foods were worth using, and how much to rely on her inherited folk experience of using natural foods and of preserving them at home against times of need or for economy.

Today, 'convenience' foods are so plentiful that eight housewives in ten, both in country and town, buy them automatically, and have almost forgotten how to use some kinds of fresh produce. We have forgotten, for instance, the old-style savoury puddings and herb breads, fresh vegetable pottages and fruit pickles. Yet fresh natural and whole foods and home preserves still, by and large, contain more balanced nourishment and have more individual flavour, aroma and colour than those in packets and cans; so we would be wise to recall some of the old, simple foods and processes, and learn how to make the best use of them. We should also learn, like the cooks in the past, how to use convenience foods sensibly to supplement natural foods, and how to make the best use of them, by adding fresh foods to extend their nutrients and add flavour.

With inflation, many of us cannot afford to buy steak and strawberries when we feel like it or to choose our meals from gourmet delicatessen and supermarket shelves. This book, therefore, is written for people who, like myself, want to eat wisely and well, but haven't the money to live luxuriously. In fact we want health, energy and first-class meals without paying for them!

This can be achieved even by busy people, by using and adapting bought goods with flair, and by adding home-craft products such as our own crusty, satisfying breads and aromatic pickles. The recipes I have chosen as examples are designed to make the most of their ingredients by conserving their nutrients, flavour and looks, and by using them economically — for instance by adding cheap products to costly ones to make them go further, and by sensible storage of foods which are in season and therefore plentiful. In these ways we can all make good-value, bargain meals which are pleasant and varied, simple or sophisticated as we choose. I hope you enjoy making them as much as I have done.

M. K. B.
London, 1981

1

GOOD PRODUCTS TO USE

—◆◇◆—

Shopping for natural products and wholefoods is getting easier all the time. Several kinds of wholemeal flour, such as self-raising and bread flour, are now being produced by mass millers for example, although a few years ago it was hard to find even plain wholemeal flour. Low-extraction flours, with only a little of the nutritious wheat germ removed, are also easy to get.

This may not seem true if you live in the country with only a few small shops nearby, or in a town where the idea of using natural foods has not made much impact. Their distribution is still patchy; but it *is* improving — especially now that supermarkets are getting bigger, and aim to cater for more sections of the public than before. Most big supermarkets now stock wholemeal pasta, and at least a few unprocessed grains and pulses in packets if no more. Health-food shops and small, Indian-run stores do so too.

In some ways, this makes it more difficult to know what to choose, even in a health-food store, and certainly in a supermarket. Even while I have been writing this book, at least three new commercially produced but 'clean' basic natural products have come onto the market. Your inclination, especially if shopping trips are infrequent, is to gather up with joy all sorts of goods when you see them, in case you cannot get them later; this is often a mistake, because many natural foods and wholefoods have a shorter shelf-life than heavily processed ones. If they go 'off peak', you will have wasted your money and products which someone else could have bought and used. Don't worry if you have to use substitutes sometimes: the occasional use of processed, even of 'junk', foods will do no harm if your overall eating pattern is sensible. Not all processed and packaged foods are harmful either; some may even be safer, healthwise, than the original thing (canned red kidney beans are one example).

To save you stocking up with a lot of different types of wholefoods and natural foods 'just in case', I have listed below the basic kinds. To make your shopping and storage easier, I have used only a fairly limited range of products. For the same reason, I have included some newish ones which you may like to know about, and which you can trust are made from natural ingredients. Not all manufacturers have to describe their products on the packaging, and the names may be useful. These are all goods which I have used personally, and have faith in.

Breadcrumbs
Use wholemeal bread for crumbs, unless your recipe specifies rye breadcrumbs. Granary and mixed-grain breads, although good to eat, do not make fine, even crumbs.

Butter or oil
Use unsalted butter if possible, or a pure vegetable oil for frying. Corn, ground-nut, safflower, sunflower or sesame oil can be used; the first two are the lightest and neither burns easily. Olive oil and walnut oil are unstable; they turn rancid and they burn easily at a low temperature, so they are not suitable. They also give their own flavour to other foods.

Canned fruits and vegetables
Don't scorn plain products in cans, such as fruits and some vegetables. Read the labels carefully. Canned fruits in natural juice may not have the vital flavour of raw fresh fruit, but can be useful for bulking it out. You will have to use canned pineapple in recipes using gelatine; fresh pineapple has a sad effect. If vegetables are labelled as canned with only salt and water they are as 'pure' as fresh, partly cooked vegetables — monotonously low in flavour perhaps but useful, like fruit, for bulking out fresh vegetables or for adding a needed touch of colour to a dish. A few chopped canned carrots, for instance, can make a dull-toned 'stir-fry' a thing of beauty.

Remember to allow for the fact that canned vegetables have already been heat-treated when you cook them. They should cook in a few moments. So, for the same reason, should frozen vegetables. Take care not to overcook them.

Chocolate
Cocoa, chocolate and sweetened drinking chocolate, in particular, are fairly heavily processed. Carob is a slightly sweet natural substitute for chocolate which comes from the nut of a small tree. However carob powder is expensive to buy, and it needs some care in handling, so I have used unsweetened cocoa in recipes in this book.

Cream
Use double or whipping cream as you wish. Double cream is richer, but whipping cream gains more volume and is less cloying (and slightly less fattening). Longlife cream (and milk) taste, at least to me, of the carton, as a result of being heated. Thick (clotted) cream in cans and jars also has this cooked flavour. As a cream substitute, evaporated milk tastes artificial, and sweetened condensed milk is so sugared it tastes of little but sweetness. Mock cream made with unsalted butter and milk in a blender is a useful cream substitute in emergencies.

[11]

Flour

Use 100 per cent wholewheat or wholemeal flour, stone-ground if possible, for general cooking. If you want a pale or slightly less flavoured product, eg a sauce for white fish, use 85 per cent or 81 per cent extraction flour.

You can get all these types in the form of plain (all-purpose) flour, self-raising flour and bread (strong) flour. If the type of self-raising flour you want is not available, use 1 teaspoon of bicarbonate of soda (baking soda) and 2 teaspoons cream of tartar per lb/450g plain flour (or 1 teaspoon cream of tartar if your recipe contains soured milk, yoghurt or lemon juice). This mixture is preferred by natural food enthusiasts to baking powder, which contains aluminium sulphate. If you cannot get bread flour, use plain (all-purpose) flour.

Fruit juices

Although labelled 'natural', juices have usually been processed by being 'reduced' to concentrates, then reconstituted. If you have a juice extractor, use it to squeeze your own orange juice. A small proportion of carrot juice will add to its bulk at small cost.

A number of fruits are now canned in natural juice instead of syrup. It can be useful, although it lacks the vibrant flavour of fresh fruit or freshly squeezed juice.

Herbs

Use fresh if possible — if using dried herbs, use half the stated quantity, unless the recipe specifies otherwise.

Pastry

Use 85 per cent or 81 per cent flour for making pastry. Frozen and packeted wholemeal pastry is not yet available, but ready-baked wholemeal pastry cases (flan cases) are made in a 6in/150mm and 8in/200mm size, and are worth searching for. They are made with pure natural products.

Rice

Use brown rice. Read the packet label carefully as reddish and other poor-quality rice is sometimes sold as brown rice. Remember that brown rice takes up to twice as long to cook as white rice and does not swell as much. Cook it gently instead of boiling it fast like white rice.

Salt

Use sea salt if you can, unless your recipe demands a very fine salt. In any case keep salt to a minimum and, unless your recipe says otherwise, only season foods with it after cooking. Don't salt vegetables before cooking, for instance. If you want to avoid using salt, use kelp powder or interesting mixed spices instead. You may easily get so used to the alternative flavour that you do not notice the loss of salt.

Sweeteners

Honey   This is a pure natural sweetener, and a better choice than most sugars and syrups. There are many different honeys, ranging from light to dark, simply sweet to strongly flavoured. Try several until you find the one you like best; or if you can afford it and are dedicated enough, keep different kinds in stock for different dishes. (This is a counsel of perfection!)

Use clear honey; it is easier to measure and handle than stiff honey. Stand the jar, opened, in a pan of hot water before use to thin it; it will then cream better with butter or eggs, for instance. To measure it by weight, put a bowl or other utensil on your scale, and note the weight. Then pour in enough honey to make the scale record the jug's weight plus the weight of honey you want.

Honey will make doughs and batters slightly moister and coarser than will sugar — reduce the quantity of other liquids slightly, to allow for it.

Sugars   Natural molasses is as pure as honey, but expensive and hard to get. Most molasses sold is synthetic or blended; instead, use the pure cane syrup now marketed by the makers of natural (unrefined) sugars.

Some natural and wholefood enthusiasts will not use sugar at all. But the natural muscovado sugars, light, medium and dark, are pure natural products. So is the new golden granulated sugar marketed by the same firm. It is particularly good if you want a light-coloured product, for instance almost transparent pickles, and its flavour is delicious in puddings and cakes. If you want a pure white product, such as a cake icing, you have to use refined white sugar; but do so as rarely as possible.

Dried fruits   These are, of course, just as natural as honey — in fact more so, since all honey except honeycomb has been de-waxed and purified. Dried fruits were the standard sweetening in the Middle Ages; even then, honey was expensive. They are not suitable for

[13]

sweetening all dishes, but they make delicious natural puddings and sweets (pages 167 and 192).

Fruit juices These can be used for sweetening a lot of dishes; use orange or apple juice instead of milk or water sometimes. Americans can add a little wine to non-alcoholic cider where various English ciders are required.

Yeast
Use fresh or dried yeast as you wish. The slight difference in method, together with the way to make a basic dough, is described on page 80.

2

MEAT AND FISH
Making the Most of Them

—◆◆—

Any meat or fish is a first-class protein food; this is because its proteins, unlike those in other foods, contain all the amino-acids which the human body needs, in the right proportions. To get the same essential 'mix' from other foods you must eat two or more of them together. In general, animal proteins also have more food value than plant proteins, so they are the best, as well as the most convenient, protein 'buy' for anyone who will eat them.

Meat and fish are, however, the most expensive protein foods, so it is worth taking trouble to choose them wisely and cook them well. For instance, fatty or gristly meat is much cheaper than a first-class grilling or roasting cut, but the quantity of useless material which you must store, cook and then discard may offset this. On the other hand, some cuts or types of meat, such as brisket or brains, are cheap either because they need a long cooking time or because people are prejudiced against them; if you can find a way round these problems, they are excellent value.

A few specialist butchers sell only naturally raised meat, but they are few and the meat is usually costly. If you eat meat, you have to come to terms with the fact that it has been raised, slaughtered and hung commercially — unless of course you confine your meat diet to small game such as wild rabbit and game birds.

[15]

Small is not beautiful where butchers' meat is concerned. A large piece of, say, topside is often cheaper, pound for pound, than a small one, and is generally moister and better flavoured after cooking. Chops and steaks are the most expensive cuts to buy, yet seldom the most succulent. However, hardly any of us now need the large household joints commonly carved by the *paterfamilias* of a Victorian household. Even people who buy a whole or half carcass for freezing have it butchered into small joints and assorted cuts before packaging it; and most of us just buy enough meat for a small family to eat at once or within a few days. If you have a freezer, stewing meat is certainly more economical if you buy and cook it in bulk. You can save fuel and hours in the kitchen, as well as shopping trips, because you can make one large, basically flavoured stew or casserole-style dish, and portion it before freezing. Then each portion can be reheated with different vegetables or herbs.

Choosing wisely, especially for use at once, means considering first and foremost what your family will like and what you will have time to cook well, not necessarily the cheapest meat. Don't risk the waste of having, say, fatty meat refused at the table. If you know it will be unpopular, it is probably a bad buy, even if it is a 'special offer' in the shop. Don't risk spoiling your meat by hurried or slapdash cooking either. If you'll be pushed for time before a meal, and aren't a dedicated pressure-cooker cook, choose offals, poultry or fish instead of expensive grilling or quick-baking cuts. Alternatively, if you have a solid-fuel stove, a slow cooker or an oven with automatic controls, use it to slow-braise or stew cheaper meat ahead of when you will need it. You can cook it overnight, for instance, as continental Catholic housewives have done for centuries, so that they have a feast dish ready after a vigil or long church service.

A microwave oven will, of course, tenderise even stubbornly coarse meat in minutes; but it does not produce the rich, nutrient-filled pan-juice gravy or the plentiful super-saving natural stock and fat which you get from naturally slow-simmered or braised meat. These are always a good bonus, like the natural aspic you get if you add a pig's trotter or veal knuckle to your stewpan.

Cheap cuts and stewing meat need more preparation than roasting or grilling meat, as well as more cooking time; so if you can afford to buy several days' supply at a time, choose some of each. Not only does this save labour — variety is important for good digestion as well as enjoyment! A sizeable, good-quality roasting joint provides a pleasant cold meal, and also makes good 'leftovers' dishes. On

these grounds, it is good economy to include at least one roasting joint in a week's supply of meat instead of buying different cheap cuts for every day.

If you buy mostly cheaper meats, you will need to vary both the types you get and the ways you handle them. If you buy ahead, an excellent way to preserve — and improve — cheap meat is to marinate it, as in the Winter Casserole on page 20. Don't only use a marinade in the conventional way for red meats and game, though. Try marinating offals in the dreg-ends of a bottle of wine (sherry for liver or kidneys), it makes a remarkable difference to them, especially to cheaper offals such as pig's liver and kidneys, which many people balk at eating. It removes the bitter flavour, making these economical, nutritious meats taste like a luxury dish, at, in fact, very small cost. It also makes them an excellent end-of-the-week meal since they *need* to marinate for at least 48 hours in the refrigerator.

Sweetbreads and brains soaked with an onion in a little white wine (or vermouth and water) benefit in much the same way; they get a firmer texture and lose their soapy flavour. You can firm them up even more by egging and crumbing, then frying them; or try cooking them like pasta in a well-flavoured Bolognese-type sauce.

Sheep's or pigs' hearts are an excellent, very cheap meat. If your family is prejudiced against them, disguise them; they can 'extend' a scanty beef or lamb casserole without being recognised.

[17]

Alternatively, roll them in aromatic dried herbs and pepper or sprinkle them with Herb Vinegar (page 144) and refrigerate them, closely wrapped, for 24 hours; they will then lose any strong flavour. Having done that, snip out any tubes and cut off the fatty tops. Then stuff them, and roll them in bacon or cabbage leaves like 'beef olives'. One of their merits is that they take kindly to almost any stuffing, from plain parsley and onion to anchovies or tangerine.

If you buy several hearts at a time, you can give them three or four different stuffings, casserole them all together, then freeze some as standby meals. Just take care to avoid insistent and garlicky stuffings. This idea makes hearts a particularly good 'buy' for anyone living alone, since each makes a good solid-meat main helping. Most bigger supermarkets now stock them frozen.

Much so-called fresh meat and wet fish has in fact been frozen or deeply chilled, and thawed. However, one advantage it has over frozen supermarket 'tray meats' and pre-packaged fish is that one can see it clearly. It is irritating, for instance, to buy a cloudy package of frozen fish fillets for two people, only to find on thawing them that the weight is made up of one grossly thick piece and one tiny tail bit. Another advantage of 'fresh' meat is that it has been professionally thawed, well within its high-quality storage life, and slowly, in a larger piece than one normally buys.

All 'tray meats' and commercially frozen fish need cooking with more care and, as a rule, more flavourings than butchers' cuts and 'wet' fish. Frozen fish, in particular, benefits from being marinated in a little spicy sauce or a flavoured vinegar (page 144) before cooking; it is then best dry-cooked by baking or grilling.

Nothing, of course, can beat the flavour and texture of freshly caught fish, but most freshwater fish are undervalued by both anglers and cooks. You have to gut and clean them yourself, and they may have a slightly muddy flavour or many tiny bones, but these last problems can be overcome by marinating and sensible cooking. Try a fish stew or a mixed-fish chowder; or use the home fisherman's catch as the French use pike, to make small fish balls. Less-than-fine fish also make good stuffings for vegetables or pancakes — and remember that bones, heads and whole 'tiddly'small fish give you beautifully, firm, natural aspic for other cold dishes.

Here are recipes showing some of the ways in which you can deal with meat and fish to get the best value from them. Don't treat these recipes as rigid instructions, however. Rather, use them just as guidelines for cooking whatever type of meat or fish you get.

[18]

MEAT

◆◇◆

BEEF AS YOU LIKE IT (Serves 10–12)

You can call this 'Boeuf à la Mode' if you prefer. Every French housewife has her own version; you vary this one by using whatever wine and flavourings you have to hand. Mrs Beeton used port wine and turnips in hers, in 1860.

4–5lb/1.8–2.3kg piece of lean braising beef (see recipe)	1 sprig thyme
	1 bay leaf
6oz/150g thin wide strips hard pork fat	8oz/200g pork rind, in one piece
	salt and pepper
2 tbsp mixed herbs (2½ tbsp)	1¼lb/600g carrots, left whole
oil and butter for greasing	¾pt/375ml dry white wine (scant 2 cups)
1 onion, sliced	
1 carrot, sliced	1¾–2¼pt/1–1.2 litres beef stock, or
1 calf's foot or veal knuckle, split	as needed (2¼–2¾pt + 2 tbsp)

Choose a solid cube-shaped piece of meat, not a thin one. Cut off excess fat, then either lard it or bard it. Larding means cutting the pork fat into thin strips and threading it through the meat with a special needle. Barding means wrapping the meat in the fat and tying it securely. Either way, coat the fat strips or whole piece with the mixed herbs first.

Grease a large baking tin with oil and flaked butter. Put in the meat, onion, carrot, calf's foot or veal knuckle, thyme and bay leaf. Place in the oven, at 400°F (200°C), Gas 6, for 8–10 minutes until the fat on the meat runs and the exposed surfaces are brown. Baste the meat with the fat and turn it over. Cook it for another 7–10 minutes or until it is well browned on all sides, together with the vegetables and bones.

While browning the meat, boil the pork rind for a few minutes, drain it and cut it into large squares. Also grease a deep casserole which will just hold the meat and other ingredients. Line the bottom and part of the sides with the rind, fat side down.

Reduce the oven to 300°F (150°C), Gas 2. Transfer the meat and other ingredients from the baking tin to the casserole. Season well. Add the whole carrots. Pour the fat out of the baking tin, put in the wine and swill it round, scraping up any solid bits, then pour the wine over the meat. Add enough stock to cover three-quarters of the meat. Seal the casserole with a tight lid, and put it in the oven for 4–6 hours; it should simmer gently all the time.

Carve as much of the meat as you want to use at once. Serve the carrots with it in a warmed serving bowl. Skim the grease off the stock, taste and boil it down for extra flavour if you wish. Add extra seasoning if needed. Use a little as a thin gravy and strain the rest for a superb jellied stock.

Variations:
1   Substitute 8oz/200g onions for 8oz/200g of the carrots.
2   Try this overnight or all-day version. Use 2 pig's trotters instead of a calf's foot or veal knuckle, and forget the pork rind. Use red wine instead of white. When you put the beef and other ingredients in the casserole, add 4–8oz/100–200g mushrooms and a seeded, chopped sweet red pepper. Squeeze half a clove of garlic over the meat if you like. Seal the casserole not only with a lid but with foil and reduce the oven to 275°F (140°C), Gas 1. Cook for 6–8 hours. Serve from the casserole — the meat will be spoon-tender. (If you cook the meat overnight, you can let it cool and reheat it for the next evening's meal, but do not take off the lid until you have done so. Reheat thoroughly for 40–50 minutes in a moderate oven.)

WINTER CASSEROLE *(Serves 4)*
A useful dish to make and freeze ahead. Use canned tomatoes unashamedly in winter and there's no harm in using a stock cube to underline flavour when you know that almost all the meat's goodness is still in the gravy. Use your own Sofa Mushrooms (page 137) to augment the root vegetables.

[20]

1¹/₂lb/700g chuck steak	1oz/25g flour (¹/₄ cup)
1 onion	15oz/425g canned tomatoes
2 carrots	1 beef stock cube, crumbled
1 bay leaf	6 tbsp water (7 tbsp)
3 tbsp malt vinegar (4 tbsp)	4oz/100g button mushrooms
salt and pepper	(1¹/₂ cups)
1 tbsp corn oil (1¹/₄ tbsp)	

Cube the meat. Skin and slice the onion. Scrape and slice the carrots. Toss in a bowl with the bay leaf, vinegar and seasoning to taste, then cover and leave for at least 4 hours. Drain and pat dry, reserving the vinegar marinade. Discard the bay leaf.

Heat the oil in a deep flameproof casserole, and fry the meat and vegetables gently for 8–10 minutes, turning until lightly browned. Stir in the flour, and cook for 2 minutes. Add the vinegar marinade, tomatoes, stock cube and water. Cover and simmer gently for 2 hours. Add the mushrooms for the last 20 minutes. Serve with boiled potatoes, and offer Herb Bread (page 84) and pickles.

BEEF COLLOPS, 1860 (Serves 4)
A quick, spicy way to cook braising beef, beloved of Victorian cooks. (Mrs Beeton used rump steak!)

1lb/450g braising beef	4 medium-sized gherkins
flour for dredging	1 tbsp capers (1¹/₄ tbsp)
butter for frying	1¹/₂ tbsp each butter and flour,
1pt/500ml beef stock (2¹/₂ cups)	blended to make beurre manié
1 shallot or spring onion,	(2 tbsp each)
including green parts	salt and pepper
1 tbsp crushed walnut pieces	
(1¹/₄ tbsp)	

Cut the meat into thin slices about 3in/7.5cm long. Dredge them with flour. Sauté them in butter quickly in a heavy saucepan or flameproof casserole, turning them until browned on both sides. Pour in the stock, lower the heat to simmering point and cover the pan. Simmer the slices until tender.

While the slices are cooking, chop the shallot or spring onion, and mix with the walnuts. Slice the gherkins thinly and add them to the mixture with the capers.

When the beef slices are just cooked, draw the pan off the heat and add the beurre manié in small spoonfuls. Stir well to melt the butter, then return to the heat and simmer until the sauce thickens. Add the onion mixture. Heat through, taste and adapt the seasoning if you wish. Serve from the casserole or turn into a warmed serving dish.

GIGOT CHOPS WITH RED CABBAGE *(Serves 4)*

This eighteenth-century supper dish is a dinner-party 'special' today. It is worth using good meat in this case, and the dish is less costly than it might be because the red cabbage is cheap.

1 small red cabbage
2 small cooking apples
2 medium onions
fat for greasing
2 tbsp muscovado sugar (2¹/₂ tbsp)
salt and pepper
1 bay leaf, 4–6 black peppercorns,
  1 sprig dried thyme, 6 parsley
  stalks, tied in a cloth
4 tbsp sweet sherry (5 tbsp)

4 slices fillet end of leg of lamb, about
  6in x 3¹/₂in/15cm x 8cm and
  ¹/₂in/1cm thick
1¹/₂pt/850ml veal or chicken stock
  (3³/₄ cups)
salt and pepper
flour for dredging
2 egg yolks
butter for frying
watercress sprigs, to garnish

Shred the red cabbage. Core and chop the apples, slice the onions. Put them all, in alternate layers, into a well-greased casserole, seasoning each layer with sugar, salt and pepper. Put the herb bundle on top; pour in the sherry and cover the casserole tightly. Bake at 300°F (150°C), Gas 2 for about 1½ hours.

Meanwhile, prepare the lamb. Trim off excess fat, and nick the edges of the slices. Put the stock in a deep frying pan (skillet) which will hold the slices in one overlapping layer. Bring to the boil. Lower the heat to simmering, and put in the lamb slices. Cover the pan, and simmer gently for 6–8 minutes or until the slices are almost cooked through and tender.

Remove the slices, pat them dry,* season and dredge them with flour. Beat the egg yolks, and brush the slices all over with egg. Fry them quickly in the butter, turning them once, until golden on both sides.

To assemble, drain the red cabbage and pile in the centre of a flat, warmed serving dish. Prop the lamb slices on end against the cabbage. Cap the red vegetable with a small bunch of green watercress sprigs just before serving.

Note: Brussels sprouts and chestnuts make a good modern alternative to red cabbage.

*To freeze:
Make ahead, cool and freeze at this point if you wish. Thaw for 2 hours at room temperature before frying.

[22]

LAMB CAKES AND APPLE *(Serves 4)*

8oz/200g minced lamb
1oz//25g fresh wholemeal
  breadcrumbs (*1/2* cup)
1 small onion, finely chopped
1 tsp powdered rosemary (1*1/4* tsp)
2 tsp Worcester sauce (2*1/2* tsp)
2 tbsp beaten egg (2*1/2* tbsp)
salt and pepper

2 sharp apples
1oz/25g golden granulated sugar
  (2 tbsp)
1/2 tsp dry mustard (*3/4* tsp)
2 tbsp buttered breadcrumbs
  (2*1/2* tbsp) see Brown Betty page 97
sauce for serving (see end of recipe)

Mix together the lamb, wholemeal breadcrumbs, onion, rosemary and Worcester sauce. Bind with the egg. Season well. Shape into 4 equal-sized patties.

Core the apples without peeling them. Cut 2 round slices through the centre of each. Lay the patties and apple slices in a single layer in a lightly greased baking tin. Mix the sugar and mustard, and sprinkle over the apple. Cover with the buttered crumbs. Bake at 350°F (180°C), Gas 4 for 35 minutes. Serve with English Brown Sauce or Brown Onion Sauce.

GRAVY KETTLE.

English Brown Sauce
(Makes 1/2pt/250ml [1 1/4 cups])
A standard accompaniment on a Victorian family dinner-table.

2 tbsp dripping or butter
  (2*1/2* tbsp)
1 small carrot, sliced
1 medium onion, sliced
2 tbsp flour (2*1/2* tbsp)

1 pt/500ml beef or strong vegetable
  stock (2*1/2* cups)
1 piece brown onion skin
salt and pepper
1 tsp sage vinegar (optional)

Melt the fat, and simmer the carrot and onion in it gently until soft and golden. Add the flour, lower the heat and stir until golden brown. Slowly stir in the stock, onion skin, seasoning and vinegar if used and simmer, uncovered, for 30 minutes. Strain before use.

Brown Onion Sauce
Use 2 onions but no carrot, and season with grated nutmeg and 1/2 tsp French mustard (3/4 tsp) as well as salt and pepper.

[23]

LAMB TURNOVERS WITH BEANS *(Serves 6)*

Meat goes further parcelled up in pancakes. The ones in this recipe look and taste delicious, being crisply fried and served with a vivid sauce and beans. Use canned beans rather than spend fuel and time on cooking just a few dried ones.

1lb/450g lean raw lamb, minced
1 rounded tbsp finely chopped
 onion (1¼ tbsp)
¼ tsp paprika (½ tsp)
1 tsp salt (1¼ tsp)
¾pt/375ml oil for frying
 (2 cups)
twelve 6in/15cm pancakes
 (not too thin)

8fl oz/200ml Home-made Tomato
 Sauce (1 cup), see end of recipe
½ tsp oregano (¾ tsp)
one 7½oz/213g can cannellini or
 butter beans, drained
4 large radishes, grated
2oz/50g grated mild hard cheese
 (½ cup)
finely shredded lettuce

Mix together the minced meat, onion, paprika and salt. Fry in a little of the oil until lightly browned. Drain. Divide the mixture between the pancakes, placing a small mound in the centre of each. Fold over the pancakes like turnovers, and secure with wooden toothpicks. Heat the remaining oil, and fry the turnovers until crisp and brown. Remove the toothpicks. Drain the turnovers on soft paper. Keep warm in a serving dish.

Heat the sauce, oregano and beans together until steaming. Turn into a warmed bowl or wide-mouthed jug. Sprinkle the radish, cheese and lettuce over the turnovers, and serve at once, with the beans in their sauce.

Home-made Tomato Sauce

1pt/500ml tomato juice (2¹/₂ cups) *¹/₄ tsp celery salt (¹/₂ tsp)*
small pinch each of ground cloves, *¹/₄ tsp Worcester sauce (¹/₂ tsp)*
pepper and cayenne pepper *¹/₂ tsp lemon juice (³/₄ tsp)*

Put all the ingredients in a heavy saucepan. Simmer, uncovered, for
25–35 minutes or until reduced to 8fl oz/200ml (1 cup). Use at once
or cool and refrigerate.

Note: You can use beef mince instead of lamb.

COLLARED BREAST OF LAMB *(Serves 4)*

'Collaring' is an old, mild way of pickling meat. An English inven-
tion, it has never been used in other countries, yet it is a simple way
to make cheap cuts tender and tasty; they will also keep for several
days in the fridge before being cooked for the table. The meat is
spiced, and flavoured with herbs and vinegar, then rolled up like an
eighteenth-century man's neckband or collar. In the old days it was
usually brined lightly or simmered in brine before being baked for
eating hot or cold.

This recipe is based on an old one which used a stuffing of 'sweet
herbs', lemon peel and spices instead of brining the meat. The only
change is the use of bottled concentrated mint instead of lemon peel
and strong spices. Besides being traditional, the vinegar counteracts
the fattiness of the lamb, and gives the meat a delicious flavour. The
alternating circles of white fat, rosy meat and vivid green make the
cheap joint a show piece when sliced.

1 boned breast of lamb, about *1 tbsp dried sliced onions, soaked and*
  2¹/₄lb/1kg before boning *drained (1¹/₄ tbsp)*
  (1¹/₂lb/700g after boning) *2 tsp chopped fresh parsley (2¹/₂ tsp)*
3 tbsp concentrated mint in *salt and pepper*
  vinegar (3¹/₂ tbsp) *butter or lamb dripping for greasing*
1 tbsp caster sugar, or to taste *and browning*
  (1¹/₄ tbsp)
1 large slice fresh bread without
  crusts, crumbled

Ask the butcher to bone the meat without cutting through the skin.
Lay the breast flat, skin-side down. Mix the concentrated mint with
the sugar and 2 tbsp (2¹/₂ tbsp) of the breadcrumbs. Spread the mixture all over the meat. Sprinkle the onions, parsley and remaining
breadcrumbs over the mint mixture, adding seasoning to taste. Roll
up the meat like a Swiss roll, and tie securely with string.

Grease a large sheet of strong foil. Wrap the meat in it. Place in a baking tin with a little water, and bake at 350°F (180°C), Gas 4 for 1–1½ hours, depending on the thickness of the meat roll. Unwrap the meat, and dot with fat. Return it to the oven, uncovered, until browned.

Serve sliced, with buttered carrots and garden peas, or with spring cabbage and butter beans.

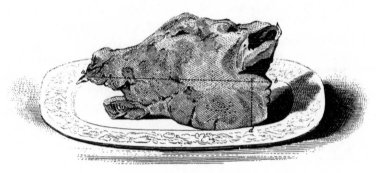

CALF'S HEAD

VEAL AND LEMON CASSEROLE *(Serves 4–6)*
Make a party dish out of this comparatively cheap meat.

1lb/450g pie veal (cubed stewing veal)
1oz/25g flour (¼ cup)
salt and pepper
3 tbsp oil for frying (4 tbsp)
1 large onion, chopped
4oz/100g button mushrooms (1½ cups)
2½–3oz/65–75g rindless streaky bacon, chopped (bacon strips)

⅓pt/150ml chicken stock (¾ cup)
⅛pt/65ml dry vermouth or white wine (⅓ cup)
1 tbsp unsweetened lemon juice (1¼ tbsp)
2 tsp honey (2½ tsp)
strip of lemon rind
2 tbsp double cream (2½ tbsp heavy cream)

Cut the veal into 1in/2.5cm cubes. Season the flour with salt and pepper, and toss the meat in it. In a flameproof casserole, fry the meat in the hot oil until well browned all over. Add the onion, mushrooms and bacon and stir over medium heat for 4 minutes.

Mix in all the remaining ingredients except the cream, and season well. Bring to the boil, then cover and transfer to the oven at 350°F (180°C), Gas 4 for 1½ hours. Stir in the cream just before serving.

PORK AND EGG PIE *(Serves 6)*

A 'hash' of meat scraps with spices is typically Victorian, although this dish is much older. You could use a proportion of canned pork luncheon meat today, to supplement scanty leftovers. Try the pressed pastry for encasing a standard veal and ham pie mixture too. It is easier to use than a conventional hot-water-crust pastry.

8oz/200g 85 per cent wholewheat flour (2 cups)
2oz/50g butter or margarine (¼ cup)
2oz/50g lard (white pork fat) (¼ cup)
3 eggs
salt and pepper
1–2 tbsp milk (1¼–2½ tbsp)

1lb/450g cooked pork, shredded (or use part or all pork luncheon meat)
2oz/50g fresh white breadcrumbs (1 cup)
pinch of onion powder
pinch each of ground mace and cloves
1 crushed coriander berry soaked in 2 tsp boiling water (2½ tsp)
4 hard-boiled eggs

Grease the inside of a 6½in/170mm loose-bottomed cake tin about 3in/75mm deep. For the pastry, shake the flour in a mixing bowl, and rub in the fats. Beat 1 egg, and put 1 tbsp (1¼ tbsp) aside for glazing. Add the rest to the dry pastry mixture with seasoning to taste. Work in, adding enough milk to make a soft dough which leaves the sides of the bowl clean.

Press the pastry evenly over the bottom and sides of the tin. Chill until firm; then line with greaseproof paper, fill with dried beans or crusts, and bake 'blind' at 375°F (190°C), Gas 5 for 15 minutes. Remove filling and bake for another 6–8 minutes.

Meanwhile, process the meat, breadcrumbs, remaining 2 raw eggs, onion powder, spices and water in a food processor or blender until pasty. Season. Chop 3 hard-boiled eggs roughly, and mix into the meat. Spoon into the pastry case. Glaze the pastry rim with the reserved beaten egg.

Bake at 350°F (180°C), Gas 4 for 40–45 minutes until the pastry is cooked and the filling firm in the centre. Leave to stand for 5 minutes, then unmould gently (if to be served hot); or cool completely before unmoulding. Chop the remaining egg and sprinkle it over the filling just before serving.

MEAT-FILLED CANNELLONI *(Serves 4)*

Use pasta, like pancakes, to make meat stretch and also to use up leftovers. Lasagne rectangles can be rolled round a meat filling to look like bought cannelloni tubes, and are easier to fill.

16–20 lasagne rectangles

FOR THE FILLING:
8oz/227g fresh or frozen chopped cooked spinach (1 cup)
12oz/300g cold roast beef or other meat
4oz/100g cooked gammon or boiled bacon
1 1/2oz/35g grated Parmesan cheese (scant 1/2 cup)
2 tbsp gravy or pan juices from meat (2 1/2 tbsp)

2 eggs
ground black pepper
1oz/25g butter (2 tbsp)

FOR THE SAUCE:
4 tbsp gravy or pan juices from meat (5 tbsp)
3/4pt/375ml thick white sauce (2 cups)
pinch of chopped fresh or dried basil
1oz/25g grated Parmesan cheese (1/4 cup)
1oz/25g butter, flaked (2 tbsp)

Bring about 3 1/2pt/2 litres (5pt) water to the boil in a large saucepan, with 2 tsp (2 1/2 tsp) salt. Drop in the lasagne rectangles, a few at a time, and boil for about 6 minutes. Take out with a slotted spoon, and put in a colander or sieve. Rinse well under cold water, then lay side by side on a wet cloth. Repeat the process to cook the remaining lasagne.

Drain the spinach thoroughly, making it as dry as possible. Mince the meats together twice or chop finely in a food processor. Put them in a bowl with the spinach, cheese and gravy or pan juices. Beat the eggs lightly and mix them in. Season with pepper.

Use the butter to grease a shallow oven-to-table baking dish which will hold the lasagne in one layer when rolled up like pancakes. Heat the oven to 400°F (200C), Gas 6.

Divide the meat filling between the lasagne rectangles, placing it in a line down one side of each. Roll up the rectangles like pancakes. Place them side by side in the dish.

Make the sauce by mixing the gravy or pan juices with the white sauce. Add the basil. Spoon over the lasagne rolls. Sprinkle with the 1oz/25g (1/4 cup) cheese, then with the flaked butter. Bake for 15–20 minutes until lightly browned. Serve very hot with a garlic-flavoured green salad.

MIXED MEAT LOAF *(Serves 4–6)*

You can make this useful standby meat loaf with beef or lamb, or with a mixture of meats including pork. Take advantage of any special offer of stewing meat to make and freeze it. It is good hot, still better if you cool it under a weight for use in packed meals. It can even double as a coarse country pâté.

1 small onion, about 2oz/50g weight	*¹/₄ tsp grated nutmeg (¹/₃ tsp)*
1 clove garlic	*¹/₄ tsp ground allspice (¹/₃ tsp)*
2 tsp dripping or margarine (1 tbsp)	*1 tsp bruised fresh thyme leaves or ¹/₂ tsp dried thyme (1¹/₄ tsp/³/₄ tsp)*
1lb/450g lean minced stewing meat	*1 tbsp finely chopped parsley (1¹/₄ tbsp)*
2oz/50g rolled oats (²/₃ cup)	*salt and pepper*
1 tbsp natural wheat bran (1¹/₄ tbsp)	*1 egg*
	milk for mixing, if needed

Chop the onion and garlic fairly finely. Fry them gently in the fat until soft but not coloured.

Mix together thoroughly the minced meat, rolled oats and bran, breaking up any meat lumps. Mix in the spices and herbs, then the onion, garlic and any fat in the frying pan. Season. Beat the egg lightly, and use it to bind the mixture, adding a little milk if needed to make it moist but not sloppy.

Grease a 7¹/₂in x 3³/₄in x 2in/190mm x 90mm x 50mm loaf tin, and put in the mixture, pressing it well down into the corners. Cover it securely with foil. Bake at 350°F (180°C), Gas 4 for 1 hour or until the loaf shrinks slightly from the sides of the tin. Pour off any free fat. Turn the loaf onto a warmed serving dish, or cool under a weight and serve sliced when cold.

PARCELLED HEARTS *(Serves 4)*

Suitable for a low-fat régime, yet interesting and flavoursome.

4 sheep's hearts	*1 tsp grated lemon rind (1¹/₄ tsp)*
4oz/100g cooked fresh spinach (¹/₂ cup)	*pinch of grated nutmeg*
2oz/50g onion	*salt and pepper*
2 thick slices of cored cooking apple, about 1oz/25g each	*Home-made Tomato Sauce (page 25)*

Cut excess fat off the hearts, and snip out interior valves, membranes and skin. Rinse the hearts inside. Shred the spinach leaves finely; chop the onion and apple. Mix them with the lemon rind, grated nutmeg and seasoning. Stuff the hearts with the mixture, and close the top openings with small poultry skewers. Wrap each heart completely in greased foil.

Drop the parcels into a pan of simmering water, and simmer for 30–40 minutes until the hearts are tender but not over-solid. Arrange them on a warmed serving dish, and coat them with Home-made Tomato Sauce.

LIVER AND BACON *(Serves 4)*

Ox or pig's liver is fine for braising, or marinating as for kidneys (opposite). But use the best liver for frying or grilling, as in this dish; it is false economy to do otherwise.

8 rindless streaky bacon rashers (8 strips)	*2 tbsp flour (2¹/2 tbsp)*
	salt and pepper
2oz/50g butter or bacon fat (¹/4 cup)	*1lb/450g slices of lamb's liver*
	hot water
2 medium onions, skinned and sliced	*lemon juice*
	chopped parsley, to garnish

Fry the bacon in a large frying pan until just crisp. Remove it, leaving any fat in the pan, and keep it warm in the oven, under foil. Add a little of the butter or fat to the pan, and fry the onions until golden brown. Add to the bacon. Season the flour, dust the liver slices with it, and fry them for 3–4 minutes on each side. Remove them to a warmed serving dish. Place the bacon on top, and the onions around them.

Stir enough hot water into the pan to make a thin gravy. Simmer for 2–3 minutes. Sprinkle the liver with gravy, lemon juice and chopped parsley. Serve at once, with the rest of the gravy and with mashed potatoes.

FAGGOTS *(Serves 4)*

A popular 'people's meal' in Victorian times.

1lb/450g pig's liver	*pinch of grated nutmeg*
3 medium onions	*wholemeal flour or fine oatmeal for coating*
salt and pepper	
3oz/75g wholemeal bread	*dripping, bacon fat or sausage fat for greasing*
4–5 tsp seasoning made up of finely chopped sage, thyme, parsley and lemon rind well seasoned with salt and pepper (5–5¹/2 tsp)	

Cut the liver and onions into small pieces. Bring a pan of water to simmering point, and add the meat and onions, with a little salt and pepper. Simmer until barely cooked; the liver should still be pink inside. Mince the meat, onions and bread together. Then pound them to a smooth paste with a little of the cooking liquid if you need it, or process them in an electric blender. Flavour them with the herb mixture suggested, or with similar herbs. Add the nutmeg. Then divide the mixture into 8 portions, form them into round balls, and roll them in the flour or oatmeal.

Grease a small baking tin generously with fat, and lay the faggots in it side by side. Cover them loosely with greased foil, and bake at 350°F (180°C), Gas 4 for 25 minutes. Take off the foil, and bake them for another 7–10 minutes. Separate them with a knife if they have stuck together. Serve very hot, with Home-made Tomato Sauce (page 25).

MARINATED KIDNEYS *(Serves 4)*
People who refuse pigs' kidneys as rank-tasting will be pleasantly surprised by this colourful, quick-to-cook dish.

4 pigs' kidneys, about 3oz/75g each	*2in/5cm piece cucumber*
1/8pt/65ml medium sherry (1/3 cup)	*1 tsp white vinegar (1 1/4 tsp)*
1 small onion, finely chopped	*8 canned apricot halves, drained*
1 young stalk celery	*1 tbsp oil for frying (1 1/4 tbsp)*
1/2 green pepper	*salt and pepper*

Put the kidneys in a shallow dish and pour the sherry over them. Add enough water to cover most of the kidney. Scatter the onion on top, and refrigerate for 24–48 hours. Turn the kidneys over once or twice, to soak both sides.

Shortly before cooking, cut the celery, pepper and cucumber into 1/4in/5mm dice, mix together and sprinkle with vinegar. Chop the apricots, not too finely.

Remove the kidneys from the marinade, but keep it. Halve the kidneys lengthways, core them, then cut them into 1/2in/1cm slices across. Heat the oil in a frying pan and sauté the kidneys until they change colour. Add the marinade, vegetables and apricots, lower the heat and simmer for 5–7 minutes until the kidneys are lightly cooked through and the sauce is slightly reduced. Season well, and serve over boiled wheat, rice or barley.

[31]

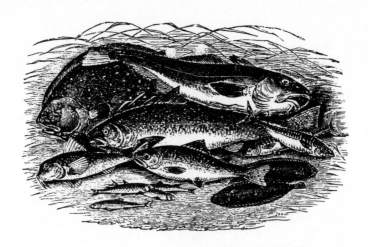

FISH

—◆◆—

MARINATED FISH KEBABS *(Serves 2, or 4 light helpings)*

You will need a whole lemon for the kebabs, but use bottled lemon juice for the marinade to cut costs. This semi-sweet, double-purpose mixture serves to glaze the fish while cooking too. It can also be used to marinate steaks, chops, liver or cubed ox-kidney before grilling or barbecuing them. *Colour picture opposite.*

FOR THE MARINADE:
3 tbsp clear honey (4 tbsp)
2 tbsp lemon juice (2¹/₂ tbsp)
1 tbsp soy sauce (1¹/₄ tbsp)
1 drop Tabasco or small pinch of
  chilli powder

FOR THE KEBABS:
3 medium mackerel or whiting,
  cleaned but not skinned
2 medium onions, cut in thin rings
4 courgettes, sliced in rounds
  1in/2.5cm thick
1 lemon, sliced in rounds

Mix the marinade ingredients in a saucepan. Warm them, and stir until blended. Keep aside.

Discard the fish heads and tails. Cut the fish across into 'steaks' 1¹/₂in/3.5cm thick. Thread fish, vegetables and lemon slices alternately on 4 skewers. Lay them in a shallow dish, and pour the marinade over them. Marinate for 20 minutes, turning once.

Heat the grill well, and place the skewers in the hot grill pan. Brush them with marinade. Grill, using medium heat and turning and brushing with marinade frequently, for about 15 minutes. Serve at once, with grilled tomatoes and couscous or brown rice.

Marinated Fish Kebabs *(Gale's Honey)*

FISH CHOWDER *(Serves 4)*
A classic American chowder, economical and good.

1lb/450g fresh haddock fillet or
*   similar white fish*
4oz/100g piece of boiling bacon
salt and pepper
8fl oz/200ml water (1 cup)

1lb/450g peeled potatoes
1 small onion, chopped
3/4pt/375ml milk (2 cups)
pinch of grated nutmeg
1 tbsp butter (1 1/4 tbsp)

Skin the fish, remove any bones, and cut into cubes. Season with salt. Cut any rind off the bacon and cut the meat into small dice.

Cut the potatoes into 1/2in/1cm cubes. Put the water and a little salt into a saucepan and add the potatoes. Cover and simmer until they are tender but not broken.

Meanwhile, fry the bacon without extra fat until golden and crisp. Remove from the pan with a slotted spoon. Fry the onion in the bacon fat until soft and lightly browned. Pour the milk into the frying pan, swirl round and stir over gentle heat for 2 minutes.

Pour the milk into the saucepan with the potatoes. Add the fish and 2 tbsp (2 1/2 tbsp) of the bacon dice. Season well with salt, pepper and nutmeg. Add the butter. Simmer the chowder gently until the fish is tender. Sprinkle the rest of the bacon dice on top and serve very hot.

CRUSTED COD CUTLETS *(Serves 4)*
Long ago, this way of covering meat or fish was called 'endoring'. It was used mostly for spit-roasted meat; but it is an excellent way of giving a flavoursome, attractive topping to often tasteless frozen fish.

2 large egg yolks
pinch of saffron strands or curry
*   powder infused in 2 tsp boiling*
*   water (2 1/2 tsp)*
good pinch of ground ginger

salt and pepper
2 tbsp flour (2 1/2 tbsp)
extra hot water if needed
4 thick cod steaks or pieces of skinned
*   cod fillet*

Beat the egg yolks well with the spiced water. Mix the ginger and a little salt and pepper into the flour, then gradually work the dry mixture into the egg yolks. Add extra hot water if needed, to make a very thick batter.

Herb Bread, page 84, Tomato and Thyme Soup, page 152, and Cheese Pots, page 166 *(Van den Bergh's Ltd)*

Grill the fish gently on both sides. Remove from the heat, and pat off any free fat or moisture. Paint or brush one side with the batter. Return to the heat, and grill gently for 2–3 minutes until the topping is crisp and golden brown.

BANDED FISH LOAF *(Serves 6–8)*

You can make even plebeian coley colourful and delicious by adding wisely chosen canned fish and the flavour of herbs. Use canned red salmon and a few canned shrimps instead of pilchards if costs allow.

3 tbsp butter (4 tbsp)
2oz/50g finely chopped mild
*   onion (¼ cup)*
1oz/25g plain flour (¼ cup)
1 tsp dried dill (1¼ tsp)
12fl oz/300ml single cream or top
*   of the milk (1½ cups)*

1½lb/700g coley or other white fish fil-
*   let, skinned and cut into small pieces*
3 eggs, beaten
salt and pepper
one 7½oz/215g can pilchards in
*   tomato sauce*
watercress sprigs, to garnish

Melt the butter in a frying pan over low heat, add the onion and stir until it softens. Add the flour and stir for 1 minute. Sprinkle in the dill. Then slowly add the cream, stirring continuously until the sauce thickens. Remove from the heat, stir in the white fish and beaten eggs, and season well.

Open the can of fish and drain well over a jug to save the sauce. Split whole fish lengthways and remove the spines. Keep aside.

Put half the white fish mixture in a food processor or blender, and process until smooth. Spread this mixture evenly in an 8in x 4in x 3in/200mm x 100mm x 75mm loaf tin. Spread the halved canned fish and any small pieces evenly on top. Process the remaining white fish mixture, and spread it over the pilchards.

Stand the tin in a baking dish and pour 1½in/35mm boiling water into the dish. Bake for 30 minutes at 350°F (180°C), Gas 4. Cool in the tin on a rack, under a light weight; then chill for 24 hours, covered, before use. Garnish with watercress sprigs and, if using pilchards, with the reserved tomato juice from the can.

COD'S HEAD

VICTORIAN STEWED TROUT *(Serves 2)*

This recipe by Eliza Acton is a pleasant way to deal with any river fish, or with oily fish such as mackerel or conger. It makes them firm and flavourful, yet moist and not too fatty.

2 medium rainbow trout or small
   mackerel
3oz/75g butter or margarine
   (1/4 cup + 2 tbsp)
1 tbsp flour (1 1/4 tbsp)
good pinch each of ground mace
   and grated nutmeg
a few grains of cayenne pepper
3/4 pt/375 ml chicken stock
   (scant 2 cups)

3 parsley sprigs
1 fresh or 1/2 dried bay leaf
1 broad strip lemon rind, thinly
   pared
1 tbsp dry white wine or dry
   vermouth (1 1/4 tbsp) (optional)
salt and pepper

Clean the fish, and cut off heads, tails and fins. Scale if needed. Rinse and wipe dry.

Melt the fat in a heavy saucepan or deep frying pan which will hold the fish side by side. Stir in the flour, spices and pepper. Put in the fish, and brown them on both sides. Add the stock, herbs, lemon rind and wine or vermouth. Bring to simmering point, reduce the heat and simmer, half-covered, for about 15 minutes or until the fish is cooked through but not soft. (The time will depend on the thickness of the fish.) Remove the fish to a warmed serving dish, and keep warm.

Skim all the fat off the liquid in the pan. Taste, and boil down rapidly for a few moments if a stronger flavour is wanted. Strain the liquid over the fish (the perfectionist Victorian cook says 'use a hot strainer'!) Serve at once with small, plainly boiled potatoes.

THE TROUT.

SEVERN CRUMBLE (Serves 4–6)
Fish is quick and therefore cheap to cook, if not to buy. River fish from an angler's bag or frozen fish can be used for this savoury crumble; use a mixture of different fish if you like.

1/2 small onion, finely chopped
1 1/2 tbsp frying oil (2 tbsp)
1 lb/450g skinned, boned trout or
    white fish, cut into small pieces
3 tbsp cooked peas (4 tbsp)
3/4pt/375ml water (2 cups)
1 tbsp white vinegar (1 1/4 tbsp)
salt and pepper

4oz/100g butter or margarine
    (1/2 cup)
6oz/150g flour (1 1/2 cups)
4oz/100g Cheddar or Cotswold
    cheese, finely grated (1 cup)
1 sharp eating apple
2 tbsp cornflour (2 1/2 tbsp cornstarch)
4 tbsp English strong cider (5 tbsp)

In a saucepan, sauté the onion in the oil until soft. Stir in the fish, peas, water, vinegar and seasoning. Cover and cook gently for 7 minutes. Meanwhile, rub the fat into the flour until it is like breadcrumbs. Mix in the cheese and season well. Peel and core the apple, and slice thinly.

Cream the cornflour with the cider. Stir it into the fish mixture, and simmer, stirring constantly, for 2–3 minutes. Season if needed. Spread half the mixture in a greased 1 1/2pt/850ml (2pt) pie dish (baking dish). Cover with a single layer of apple slices, then with the remaining fish mixture. Spread the cheese crumble mixture on top.

Bake at 350°F (180°C), Gas 4 for 15 minutes. Raise the heat to 425°F (220°C), Gas 7 and bake for 5–7 minutes longer until the crumble is crisp and golden.

[38]

FISH AND 'CHIP' CASSEROLE *(Serves 4)*

It may seem strange to mix fish and meat, but it's not unknown, and the spicy taste of sausage helps the sometimes drab flavour of white fish.

4 white fish cutlets or solid pieces,
*   about 6oz/150g each*
2 onions, about 6oz/150g each
5oz/125g mushrooms
1/4pt/125ml tomato juice
*   (1/2 cup + 2 tbsp)*

a few drops of Worcester sauce
1 tsp dried marjoram (1 1/4 tsp)
salt and pepper
4 cooked chipolata sausages

Trim any fins or ragged skin off the fish and pack the pieces side by side in a greased ovenproof casserole. Skin the onions, and chop them finely with the mushrooms. Add both to the casserole. Mix the tomato juice with the Worcester sauce and marjoram. Pour it over the contents of the casserole, and season to taste. Cover tightly.

Bake at 325°F (160°C), Gas 3 for 20–25 minutes until the fish is tender. After the first 10 minutes, add the chipolata sausages, cut into 1/2in/1cm pieces. When the fish is cooked, serve at once, very hot.

3

GOOD VALUE
Poultry and Small Game

———◆◆◆———

It is not long since chicken and, especially, turkey were Sunday dinner or feast-day fare, but now they are among the cheapest meats
you can buy. Fresh birds cost more than frozen, oven-ready ones,
but are still good value compared with red meat. Joints or quarters
cost slightly more than a whole bird of the same size, and for a
household a whole chicken is better value. It can be jointed in
moments; the giblets, usually included, are valuable for stuffing or
stock; and the carcass carries meat scraps and also makes good jellied
stock. When buying chicken quarters, you often pay for the bone
yet you seldom use it.

Fresh birds have firmer flesh on the whole, and naturally taste
better, especially if you get one from a farm or your personal
butcher/poulterer, still untrussed. You can hang it for a day to develop still more flavour. Draw the bird before hanging it, or ask the
poulterer to do it. Hang it by the feet with its head in a plastic bag, in
a cool, dry place. Dust it with white pepper and wrap it loosely in
muslin (an old net curtain will do).

Don't scorn frozen birds. For hundreds of years, cooks have relied on having one reliable mild meat to carry the assorted sauces and
other flavourings they took pride in making. In medieval times,
pounded chicken flesh was a standard thickener for sauces and cus-

tards, and was the basis of many savoury dishes, besides being used to 'stretch' more costly meats. It is just as valuable for all these uses today, so frozen birds can serve you well in a dozen ways besides just being eaten as roasted or grilled chicken. If you want to try old ways of cooking them, look at Victorian cookbooks such as Mrs Beeton's, both at the poultry sections and at the ways of cooking veal (which was the main mild white meat alternative of those days).

Frozen poultry really does benefit from slow thawing, and is good when cooked in dryish ways with a flavouring of spices. Barbecuing and spit-roasting are suitable methods if you have the equipment. Try putting fresh chopped herbs or a thin layer of non-starchy stuffing between the skin and flesh before roasting; the skin on frozen birds is usually quite easy to lift. Stuffing the breast of a whole chicken this way gives the bird a splendidly plump look, and adds to its food value as well as its flavour. Another way to make the most of frozen birds is, in fact, to take the skin off. This gives you several advantages. A skinned bird or pieces are less fatty, so you get dryer meat for sauced dishes; baste it with flavoured fat from a roast if you are grilling or roasting it plainly. A skinned bird is much easier to coat, too: egg and crumbs or flour stick on better. So do more exotic coverings, like the marmalade one on page 46.

As yet another bonus, the skin you remove is a good food product in its own right. Cut it in narrow strips, and lay these flat in a baking tin. Bake them when you have the oven hot for other cooking, at about 375°F (190°C), Gas 5 for 10–15 minutes or until crisp. Drain them in a round-bottomed sieve over a bowl. You will get fine pure chicken fat for cooking; and if you salt or lightly spice the crisp poultry skin while hot, it makes super cocktail snacks or a savoury crumble topping. Ideal for carbohydrate watchers, and costing not a penny!

Another way to use all parts of a bird to advantage is to stuff or 'devil' the drumsticks before or after cooking, in good Victorian style. (Use this idea, as the Victorians did, for game birds too. You will find a piece on 'devils' on page 182.)

Do try to use carcass and other chicken bones for stock; stock cubes although useful don't give you the lovely jellied stock that a real bird does. It makes an excellent soup in summer, say with diced cucumber and snipped chives folded in, and it gives flavourful body to velouté-style sauces along with extra nutrient value.

As for solid meat, remember the value of poultry (both the white and dark meat) for quiche, pancake and patty fillings, and as the solid element in stuffings (again, for carbohydrate avoiders). You can use raw meat or cooked leftovers, so every scrap of your bird can feed you.

One last thought. If you are giving a dinner party or have a family to feed, remember that a modern small turkey is not much bigger than the old-fashioned capons and boiling fowls of the past, and can be cooked in the same varied low-calorie ways, based on boiling. It is then ideal as a 'carrier' for an exotic sauce; and since it is not expensive itself, you can afford interesting sauce ingredients and a fanciful garnish. Alternatively if you want to roast it, try carving it in the kitchen, which saves time at table and lets everyone get hot meat. Present it, especially for a party, in the French style: use the stripped carcass of the lower half (the back), which is boat-shaped, as a 'canoe' in which the carved pieces are piled, mixed with small fruits or vegetables as garnish; or turn it upside-down on the serving dish and arrange the carved pieces and slices dramatically on top. You can make it a really showy dish if you have a flair for design.

CHICKEN AND TURKEY

—◆◆—

MRS GLASSE'S FOWL IN JELLY *(Serves 6–8)*

Since it shrinks much less than a roast bird, this old way of cooking
gives you plenty of firm chicken meat. If you portion it after cooking, for a sauced dish or packed meals, don't forget to scrape the
good meat off the underside of the carcass.

4lb/1.8kg boiling fowl
split veal knuckle or a few bones
salt and pepper
1 onion, split in half
2 blades mace
1/2 tsp grated nutmeg (3/4 tsp)

6–8 black peppercorns
1 strip lemon rind
lemon or orange juice to taste
white and shell of 1 egg
gravy browning (optional)
anchovy butter (page 74) (optional)

Prepare the fowl by removing excess fat and tying the legs and wings
to the body. Place in a stewpan with the veal knuckle, and just cover
with water. Bring to simmering point, and skim thoroughly. Season
the stock lightly, and add the onion, mace, nutmeg, peppercorns
and lemon rind. Half cover, and cook gently for 1½ hours or until
the thigh juices run clear when pricked with a skewer. Taste the
stock, add a little extra salt and 2–4 tsp (3–5 tsp) lemon or orange
juice. Simmer for 8–10 minutes more. Lift the bird out of the stock,
up-ending it to drain its inside. Put it aside, covered with soft paper
or a cloth, to cool. When tepid, skin it. Cool completely before you
portion it.

Raise the heat under the pan, and boil the stock until well reduced. Strain ¾–1pt/400–500ml (2–2½ cups) of the stock into a clean pan. Skim off any fat. Beat the egg white until frothy, crush the shell, and add both to the stock. Heat, whisking, until the egg white begins to set. Stop whisking. Bring to simmering point, and simmer gently for 10–15 minutes. Take care not to let bubbles break up the egg-white crust which forms.

Scald a clean jelly bag. Very gently, tip the stock into the bag and let it drip through. If not clear, drip the stock through the bag again. If using gravy browning, tint the cleared stock a rich brown while still warm. Cool. When cold but not yet set, pour a little onto a plate to test its setting quality; it should set firmly. Brush layers of the glaze over the whole or portioned bird.

Shortly before you need it, you can pipe lines or rosettes of Anchovy Butter in a decorative pattern on the bird's breast. This easy way of garnishing it comes from another recipe of Mrs Glasse's.

Note: If the stock does not set firmly, dissolve a little gelatine in a few spoonfuls of it, then whisk this into the main stock.

LEMON-BAKED CHICKEN WITH CRISPS *(Serves 4)*

*two 8–9oz/200–225g chicken
    quarters, thawed if frozen; or
    6oz/150g chicken leg joints*
½pt/250ml water (1¼ cups)
1½ chicken stock cubes
juice of 1 lemon
1 large or 2 small carrots
2 stalks celery
*1 large or 2 small green peppers,
    cored and seeded*

1 large or 2 small tomatoes, sliced
salt and pepper
chopped parsley

FOR THE CRISPS:
chicken skin
salt and pepper
*sprinkling of ground ginger or
    paprika*

Heat the oven to 350°F (180°C), Gas 4. Skin the chicken pieces, and keep the skin for the crisps. Cut the quarters or joints into 2 pieces each for serving (eg thigh and drumstick). Have ready an oven-to-table casserole with a lid.

Heat the water in a saucepan, crumble in the stock cubes, and add the lemon juice. Grate the carrot, chop the celery and the pepper flesh, put them into the casserole, and pour the hot stock over them. Season well. Lay the chicken joints on top, and cover them with the sliced tomato, and with chopped parsley. Season again. Cover the casserole tightly. Bake for 35–40 minutes, or until the chicken is tender when pierced with a skewer.

[44]

Make the crisps as soon as you put the chicken in the oven.

When the chicken is ready, serve it from the casserole, and scatter a few hot crisps over each helping to garnish it. They provide fat as well as crunchy texture.

Chicken Crisps

Cut the chicken skin into strips about ½in/1cm wide and 3in/7.5cm long. Put them in fairly neat rows in a baking tin and bake on the oven shelf above the casserole at 350°F (180°C), Gas 4 for 20 minutes, or until crisp. Drain off the fat (keep it for frying) and sprinkle the crisps with the seasoning while still hot.

Note: If you wish, cool the crisps, refrigerate or freeze them, then reheat them for use as cocktail snacks.

CIDERED CHICKEN CASSEROLE *(Serves 4)*

4 chicken quarters, thawed if frozen	¼–½pt/125–250ml chicken stock (can be from cube) (¾–1¼ cups)
2oz/50g butter (¼ cup)	8oz/200g button onions, skinned
1 onion, chopped	8oz/200g young carrots, scraped
1oz/25g flour (¼ cup)	8oz/200g shelled fresh or frozen
½pt/250ml dry cider (1¼ cups)	garden peas

Cut excess skin and fat off the chicken pieces. Melt the butter in a deep flameproof casserole, and fry the chicken until golden on all sides. Remove with tongs or a slotted spoon. Put the chopped onion in the casserole, and fry until soft and golden. Sprinkle in the flour, stir round and cook for 1 minute. Gradually stir in the cider and stock. Cook for 1 minute.

Return the chicken to the casserole with the button onions and carrots. Cover, lower the heat and simmer for 1 hour or until chicken and vegetables are tender. Twenty minutes before serving, add the peas — do not add before freezing.

To freeze:
Put the completed dish in a foil container, and cool. Cover, seal and label. Freeze for not more than 2 months. To serve, remove lid from container, cover frozen dish loosely with foil and put in the oven at 375°F (190°C), Gas 5 for ¾–1 hour. Stir in the peas 20 minutes before serving.

SESAME CHICKEN *(Serves 4)*

4 chicken breasts or turkey breast
   fillets, about 5oz/125g each
oil for brushing
1/2 tsp ground black pepper (3/4 tsp)
2oz/50g fine-cut orange
   marmalade (not jelly marmalade)
   or sweet pickle (1/4 cup)

2 tbsp sesame seeds (2 1/2 tbsp)
2 tsp natural wheat bran (2 1/2 tsp)
orange rind, thinly pared and cut into
   matchsticks
watercress sprigs

Thaw the chicken or turkey pieces if frozen. Skin them, then wipe and dry well. Brush with oil on both sides. Grill, fleshy side up, under gentle heat for 15–20 minutes, brushing once or twice with oil if they become dry. Turn, and grill for another 8–12 minutes or until cooked through. Remove from the heat.

Turn the pieces over. Season the fleshy side of each piece lightly with pepper, then spread with marmalade or pickle. Mix the seeds and bran, and sprinkle over the pieces. Dab with oil. Return to the heat, and grill gently for 4 minutes, without burning the coating.

Serve garnished with a few vivid orange 'matchsticks' and with watercress sprigs. Good on a bed of hot brown rice.

CHICKEN BASKETS *(Serves 8 buffet-style)*

Chicken goes a long way as a filling for pastry tartlets. These become a party dish just by using the eighteenth-century trick of making half-hoops of pastry to turn them into baskets. Use tiny watercress or parsley sprigs as 'flowers'.

12oz/300g short crust pastry
1lb/450g cooked white chicken
   meat without skin
2oz/50g shredded suet (1/4 cup)
1 large slice bread without crusts
1 tbsp finely chopped parsley
   (1 1/2 tbsp)
1/2 tsp grated lemon rind (3/4 tsp)

pinch of grated nutmeg
salt and pepper
1oz/25g butter, softened (2 tbsp)
1oz/25g flour (1/4 cup)
1/2pt/250ml strong chicken stock,
   strained (1 1/4 cups)
8 tiny watercress or parsley sprigs

Reserving enough pastry for 'basket' handles, line eight 2 3/4in/75-80mm well-greased deep bun tins. Cut reserved pastry into 10 strips (allowing for perhaps 2 to break). Bend the strips into semi-circles with the ends almost as wide apart as the diameter of the 'baskets'. Lay them on a greased baking sheet. Bake the cases and handles 'blind' until fully cooked and firm.

Meanwhile make the filling. Mince or pound together the chicken meat, suet, bread, parsley, lemon rind, nutmeg and seasoning (use a food processor if you have one). Blend the butter and flour together. Heat the stock almost to boiling point; remove from the heat and stir in the butter-flour mixture by spoonfuls. Stir until melted. Return the sauce to the heat, and stir until it is thick. Add the meat mixture and heat through well, stirring constantly. Reduce the heat to very low, and keep warm while assembling the cases.

Place the cases on a warmed serving dish. They should be hot, reheated briefly in the oven under greased paper if pre-cooked. Pile the chicken mixture in the 'baskets'. Set a handle upright in each 'basket', then place a tiny green sprig in the centre of each. Serve at once.

DORKINGS.

CHICKEN SALAD WHEEL *(Serves 4–6)*

This way of preparing a chicken salad makes the meat go further than if you serve a solid piece to each person. It looks delicious too, like a vari-coloured wheel. You can use other salad ingredients instead of those given provided they contrast well in colour.

1 cooked chicken breast, cut in thin slices (4¹/₂–5oz/110-125g)
2 small red-skinned apples
lemon juice
2 cooked chicken drumsticks, boned
4 large spring-onion bulbs

4 hard-boiled eggs
3–4 stalks celery, split lengthways
2 large pickled gherkins, about 2¹/₂in/6.5cm long
8oz/200g cooked beetroot
watercress for garnishing
French dressing

Have ready a large flat platter about 14in/350mm in diameter. Arrange the chicken breast slices in the middle.

Core the apples without peeling, dice and dip in lemon juice. Dice the drumstick meat. Slice the spring-onion bulbs into fine rings. Chop the eggs. Slice the celery, gherkins and beetroot.

Arrange the drained apple dice, chicken-drumstick meat, chopped eggs, beetroot and celery in 5 wedges round the white chicken meat with each item touching so that the platter is covered. Sprinkle the sliced onion on the drumstick meat, and the gherkin on the celery. Garnish with watercress and serve dressing separately.

[47]

COUNTRY CHICKEN AND MUSHROOM PÂTÉ *(Serves 6–8)*

6 rindless streaky bacon rashers
  (6 strips)
1lb/450g raw chicken meat
4oz/100g raw lean pork
4oz/100g pork sausage meat
6oz/150g button mushrooms,
  chopped (3/4 cup)

1 1/2oz/35g fresh white breadcrumbs
  (3/4 cup)
1/2 small onion
1 large tomato
1 1/2 tsp dried mixed herbs (2 tsp)
1 egg, beaten
salt and pepper

Mince coarsely 2 bacon rashers (strips), the chicken and pork. In a bowl, mix the minced meats, sausage meat, mushrooms and breadcrumbs. Chop and add the onion and tomato. Sprinkle with herbs. Mix thoroughly, and bind with egg. Season well.

Grease a deep oven-to-table baking dish, or a 7¼in x 3in x 3in/ 180mm x 75mm x 75mm loaf tin, and lay the remaining bacon rashers in the bottom. Spread the pâté mixture evenly on top. Cover securely. Stand the dish in a baking tin containing ½in/10mm depth of cold water. Bake at 325°F (160°C), Gas 3 for 1¼ hours. Pour off excess fat and leave in a cold place under a light weight until fully cooled. Then turn out and refrigerate or freeze until needed.

Serve with home-made bread (no butter) and a plain green salad.

GEORGIAN POULTRY LIVERS *(Serves 2–3)*

This must be almost the quickest and easiest main dish on record, besides being hard to beat for concentrated nourishment. It's worth making whenever you invest in a turkey for roasting; you should always be able to get frozen chicken livers these days. An average-sized turkey liver weighs 3–4oz/75–100g, but one from a large, unfrozen bird may weigh up to 6oz/150g.

1 medium to large turkey liver
butter or turkey fat for greasing
6 chicken livers
6 fl oz/150ml strong chicken stock
  (³/4 cup)
2 tbsp finely chopped mushrooms
  (2¹/2 tbsp)

few drops of mushroom ketchup
  (optional)
1 rounded tbsp butter (1¹/2 tbsp)
2 tsp flour (1 tbsp)
salt and pepper
thin slices of lemon

Enclose the turkey liver completely in a parcel of foil greased with butter or turkey fat.

Put the chicken livers in a saucepan with the stock, mushrooms and a little ketchup to taste. Blend the butter and flour to a paste and keep at hand. Bring the chicken mixture almost to the boil, then remove from the heat and stir in the butter-flour mixture by spoonfuls. When melted and blended in, return the pan to the heat and simmer for 8 minutes or until the livers are lightly cooked and the sauce thickened.

While preparing the chicken livers, place the turkey-liver parcel under modest grilling heat. Cook for 10–15 minutes, turning the parcel over once.

Open the parcel over a well-warmed serving plate and tip out the turkey liver and any juices with it. Remove the chicken livers from the sauce with a slotted spoon, and arrange them round the turkey liver. Check the sauce for seasoning, and pour over the dish. Garnish with lemon slices.

THE MUSHROOM.

[49]

CHICKEN LIVER PÂTÉ *(Serves 6)*

2 medium onions, finely chopped
2 cloves garlic, crushed (optional)
4oz/100g butter (1/2 cup)
1lb/450g chicken livers, thawed
 if frozen

salt and pepper
pinch of dried thyme
1 parsley sprig (whole)
1 bay leaf
2 tbsp brandy (2 1/2 tbsp)

Simmer the onion and garlic in half the butter until soft but not col-oured. Mix in the livers, season and add the herbs. Continue sim-mering, stirring and turning over the livers from time to time, for about 8 minutes or until they are lightly cooked through. Remove the parsley sprig and bay leaf.

Melt the remaining butter with the brandy. Put all the ingredients in a food processor or electric blender, and process until smooth. Put in a serving dish, cover and chill until needed.

CHICKEN OR TURKEY GIBLET SOUP *(Serves 4)*

Keep the poultry livers for the recipe on page 49, or use them to fill an omelette or to add flavour to dumplings or a stuffing. They are rich and delicate, and pig's liver is just as good for soup-making.

1 set turkey giblets or 3 sets chicken
 giblets without livers
4oz/100g pig's liver, cut in small
 pieces
1 3/4 pt/1 litre water (4 1/2 cups)
1 tsp lemon juice (1 1/4 tsp)
1/2 tsp sugar (3/4 tsp)
1 onion, halved
1 carrot, thickly sliced

1 stalk celery, cut in 1/2 in/1 cm pieces
fresh or dried sprigs of well-flavoured
 herbs such as thyme, marjoram,
 and basil, tied in a cloth with
 6 black peppercorns
1 bay leaf
salt to taste
1oz/25g margarine (2 tbsp)
1oz/25g flour (1/4 cup)

Clean and rinse the giblets. Put in a pan with the liver, water and lemon juice, and bring to simmering point. Skim well. Add the sugar, vegetables, herb bundle, bay leaf and salt. Cover tightly and simmer gently for 1 hour, then strain, reserving the solids.

Melt the fat in a small pan, add the flour and cook together gently until browned, stirring well. Mix in gradually enough of the soup to make a thin smooth cream, then add the mixture to the soup. Sim-mer for 6–7 minutes. Chop finely any good bits of meat and vege-table among the solids and stir them into the soup. Taste and season if needed. Serve very hot, with dripping toast (page 101).

Cabbage and Seed Salad, page 122, Broccoli Salad, page 122, and Jellied Crown Salad, page 126, filled with Imperial Russian Salad, page 134 *(Jif Lemon Juice)*

Courgettes
August 1980

Corn
on the cob
August 1980

DUCK AND PIGEON

——◆◇◆——

Duck, in spite of popular myth, is good value compared with similar-flavoured game meat if properly handled. It provides rich by-products and for a festive meal, for instance at Christmas, a small household may well find a duck more economical than other traditional meats.

A good dryish stuffing makes a duck's meat go a long way; so does the French idea of carving it in the kitchen, where you need not worry about doing it elegantly and can cut thinner slices. If you do this, try the serving method in the Pomander Duck recipe on page 55.

AYLESBURY DUCKS.

This is a celebration dinner recipe, so I suggest that, for once, you use store-cupboard foods unashamedly to make the stuffing, saving last-minute shopping and work. A fresh stuffing takes valuable time and effort to make on 'the day', yet can be hazardous if made ahead and stored.

Every scrap of a duck can be used or stored conveniently. Its broken carcass, being a good deal smaller than a turkey's, can be fitted into a medium-sized pot for soup-making. The rich fat can be frozen — a little of it makes food taste luxurious; use it instead of dripping, for instance, for basting and braising dry foods or for making omelettes. Its skin makes ideal cocktail crisps; use the recipe for making Chicken Crisps on page 45. As for its giblets, they make wonderful soups.

Duck is rich enough to suffer nothing from being commercially frozen, so you need not take any special care in cooking a frozen bird; like all birds, however, a frozen one should be thawed naturally and slowly.

Ratatouille page 139 *(Van den Bergh's Ltd)*

[53]

Pigeons, whether home-shot or bought, are the most convenient of the small birds to cook, as well as the cheapest. They were the peasant's and poacher's favourite for this reason. A fat wood-pigeon makes a comfortable meal for one person, whether cooked over the coals, in the ashes or in a pot. The last is usually the best way, since it prevents the birds drying out, and it is certainly the most adaptable. It is worthwhile for even a person living alone to process three or four at once for casseroling. As with sheeps' or pigs' hearts (page 18), you can give them different stuffings, casserole them all together, then cool, package and freeze those you want to reheat later; freeze the stock separately, or use beef, pheasant or game stock for the reheats.

WOOD-PIGEON.

It is wise to casserole home-shot wood pigeons since their age and past lifestyle are uncertain. If you get several at once, you can casserole them unstuffed, then strip the meat off the bones and use or freeze it for a pie or the eighteenth-century dish called a pupton on page 59 (one of the best recipes to use up bits and pieces I know). Make sure you get rid of the small thin rib and wing bones: they make portioning the dish difficult since they may splinter, and they are perilous to eat.

Wild pigeons should usually be hung for a day or two after being shot. Then leave them for several hours at least, if you can, in a mild marinade. Unless you have a special sauce in mind, the marinade can usually be added to the casserole.

A recipe for 4 casseroled stuffed pigeons will usually do equally well for a brace of none-too-young pheasants. They will need cooking for 15–30 minutes longer, that's all.

POMANDER DUCK *(Serves 4)*

This variation of the classic Duck with Orange makes an ideal celebration or dinner-party dish. You could add extra glamour at little
cost by moistening the stuffing and flaming the bird with a miniature
bottle of orange liqueur.

Allow 10 minutes longer than usual for dishing up, to give time
for carving and dressing the bird.

1 oven-ready duck, about 4¹/₂lb/
  2kg weight, thawed if frozen
duck fat or butter for basting

FOR THE STUFFING:
15oz/425g can butter beans
1 tbsp dried sliced onions (1¹/₄ tbsp)
1 tbsp dried mixed peppers
  (1¹/₄ tbsp)
1 tbsp finely chopped parsley
  (1¹/₄ tbsp)

1–2 small oranges
good pinch of mixed spice
salt and ground black pepper
2 tsp orange or canned apricot juice, or
  orange or apricot liqueur (2¹/₂ tsp)

FOR THE GARNISH:
15oz/425g can apricot halves in
  natural juice (optional)
1 small orange

Make the stuffing first. Drain the beans and mash thoroughly in a
bowl. Mix in the dried vegetables and parsley; you need not soak
them. Grate in the yellow rind of the orange or oranges. Remove all
pith and pips, and snip the flesh into small bits with scissors. Add
the fruit to the bean stuffing. Season with spice, salt and pepper and
moisten with fruit juice or liqueur. Mix well.

Remove any giblets from the duck. Fill it with the stuffing and
truss for roasting. Prick the skin well. Place the bird on a rack in a
roasting tin (pan) holding about ¹/₄in/5mm depth of water. Spread
lightly with fat. Roast at 350°F (180°C), Gas 4 for 1¹/₂ hours or until
tender, basting occasionally. Remove the bird from the oven and let
it rest at room temperature for a few minutes.

While roasting the duck, heat through the canned fruit for the garnish, if used. Peel the small orange, and remove every scrap of skin
to expose the bright orange flesh.

Carve the bird. Remove the legs and wings, cut the meat off them
and keep it warm. Then cut off all the breast meat on each side in
small thin slices; keep them warm too. With sharp kitchen scissors,
snip all round the carcass, cutting through the thin lower rib bones,
so that you can lift off the whole bare top of the carcass in one piece.
This will leave you with the lower (back) half of the carcass, shaped
like a boat, filled with the mounded stuffing.

[55]

Now work quickly. Put the stuffed duck 'boat' on a warmed serving dish, stuffing side up, and pile the carved breast and leg meat on top of the stuffing, leaving a space in the centre. Put the peeled orange in the space and cap it with a canned apricot half if used. Drain the rest of the warmed apricot halves and arrange them round the duck to cover the patches where you removed the legs and wings. You can stick them to the sides with cocktail sticks if you like, to make the dish look like a Viking longship.

For festival glamour, warm a miniature bottle of orange or apricot liqueur; pour it over the duck and light it just when you are ready to serve.

CIDERED PIGEONS *(Serves 2 or 4)*

The farm cook who told me this old recipe maintained that half a pigeon per person was enough, but most people can easily manage a whole one. To cook 4 pigeons, double all the ingredient quantities except the cider and stock. You will need only about 1½pt/850ml liquid.

2 fat pigeons
1¹/₂oz/35g good dripping (3 tbsp)
2oz/50g onion, thinly sliced
1 medium cooking apple, peeled,
   cored and sliced
1oz/25g flour (¹/₄ cup)
¹/₄pt/125ml chicken stock
   (¹/₂ cup + 2 tbsp)
¹/₄pt/125ml dry still cider
   (¹/₂ cup + 2 tbsp)

salt and freshly ground black pepper
sprigs of thyme, parsley and rosemary,
   fresh if possible, tied in a cloth
2 thick rashers unsmoked bacon
   (2 strips)
2 sharp eating apples, peeled and
   cored
4 slices bread without crusts
butter for spreading and frying
chopped parsley

Pat the pigeons dry after plucking and cleaning. Heat the dripping in a heavy flameproof casserole. Brown the pigeons on all sides in the fat and lift out.

Sauté the sliced onion and cooking apple gently in the same fat until soft. Add the flour and cook for a few moments, stirring all the time to prevent it sticking. Gradually stir in the stock and cider. Season well. Bring slowly to the boil.

When on the boil, add the herb bundle and replace the pigeons. Cover tightly, and put into a cool oven at 300°F (150°C), Gas 2. Cook for 1–1½ hours depending on the age and toughness of the pigeons. An hour is usually enough.

While the birds are cooking, cut the bacon rashers (strips) in half across and slice the eating apples in rings. Butter the bread slices on both sides. Grill the bacon lightly, and fry the apple and bread slices in a well-buttered frying pan until golden (or put them all in a baking tin in the oven, above the casserole, and 'bake-fry' them).

Lift out the pigeons and keep warm. Remove the herb bundle. Reduce the sauce by rapid boiling to thicken it if necessary; mine is usually thick enough. Season it if needed. Halve the pigeons lengthways. Put the fried bread slices on a warmed serving dish, and place half a pigeon on each slice. Pour a little sauce over them, and garnish the dish with apple rings and bacon. Sprinkle with chopped parsley. Serve the remaining sauce separately.

ROAST STUFFED PIGEONS, 1747 *(Serves 4)*
This old method of stuffing birds under the skin is much easier than it sounds. It not only makes the meat go further but makes the pigeons look plump and delicious. Use it also for a chicken or, especially, duck. Being dryish, the stuffing will absorb fat without becoming soggy.

4 young pigeons
flour for dredging
duck or chicken fat for basting
2 tsp finely chopped or grated
lemon peel, as garnish (2¹/₂ tsp)

FOR THE STUFFING:
the pigeon livers
2–3oz/50–75g shredded suet
(¹/₄–¹/₃ cup)
2–3oz/50–75g fresh white
breadcrumbs (1–1¹/₂ cups)
1–2 hard-boiled eggs

good pinch each of ground mace and
grated nutmeg
salt and black pepper
¹/₂ tsp chopped fresh thyme or basil or
dried savory, or to taste (³/₄ tsp or as
needed)
1 egg yolk

FOR THE SAUCE:
chicken stock as needed (see method)
2 tbsp butter (2¹/₂ tbsp)
2 tbsp flour (2¹/₂ tbsp)

With the tip of a sharp-pointed knife, loosen the skin of the pigeons from the flesh, working from the vent end. Loosen it from the whole breast on each side if possible.

Now make the stuffing (the exact quantity needed will depend on the size of the 'pockets' under the skin, but any not used can be added to the gravy). In a food processor, blend together the livers, suet, breadcrumbs, hard-boiled egg(s), seasonings and herbs, and bind to a smooth paste with the egg yolk. (Alternatively mince the eggs and livers in a food mill, then pound all the ingredients together in a mortar.)

With a rounded knife blade, fill the 'pockets' between the skin and

[57]

flesh of the birds with stuffing. Do not stretch the skin too tightly, but give the birds a smooth plump look. Tie or skewer their legs tightly together to hold in the stuffing. Dredge the birds lightly with flour, smear with fat and roast on a rack in a roasting tin for 25–35 minutes at 375°F (190°C), Gas 5. Baste with fat often while roasting. When the birds are tender, remove to a warmed serving dish. Keep them warm under buttered paper.

Make the sauce. Degrease the juices in the roasting tin, and mix in enough chicken stock to make about 12fl oz/300ml liquid (1½ cups). Add any leftover stuffing and season well. Blend together the butter and flour, making beurre manié. Bring the sauce to the boil, remove from the heat and stir in the beurre manié by spoonfuls. When it melts, return to the heat and stir until the sauce thickens. Strain the sauce over the birds and sprinkle with lemon peel.

FANTAIL PIGEONS.

MANDARINE PIGEONS *(Serves 4)*
This is a cheerfully vivid dish as well as a healthful one with its celery-rice stuffing and mandarine garnish. Like the Pomander Duck (page 55), you could turn it into a showy dinner-party dish at little expense by flaming the pigeons with orange liqueur after browning them.

5 tbsp butter or margarine (6 tbsp) *salt and black pepper*
2 onions, thinly sliced *4 pigeons*
1 stalk celery, chopped *4 tbsp game or beef stock (5 tbsp)*
4 pigeons' livers, chopped *3 mandarine oranges*
6oz/150g cooked brown rice (1 cup) *1 tsp sugar (1¼ tsp)*
2 tsp chopped parsley (2½ tsp) *watercress or sprigs of parsley*
1 strip mandarine orange rind, *(optional)*
finely chopped

Heat 2 tbsp (2½ tbsp) butter or margarine in a flameproof casserole. Sauté the onions gently in the fat until soft. Mix in the celery, livers, rice, parsley and rind, and turn over until well mixed and coated with fat. Season. Spoon the mixture into the pigeons.

[58]

Add the remaining fat to the casserole and, when heated, brown the pigeons all over. Add the stock, and cover the casserole tightly. Simmer for 15–20 minutes, shaking the casserole occasionally. Meanwhile, peel the mandarine oranges, and remove all skin, pith and pips, then divide into segments. Sprinkle with sugar. Add the segments to the casserole, with a little extra stock if needed to prevent drying out. Cook gently for another 25–35 minutes or until the pigeons are tender.

Garnish each helping with sprigs of bright green watercress or parsley, especially for a party.

PUPTON OF PIGEONS OR TURKEY *(Serves 4–6)*

Pigeons were the small birds most often used in the old days for this glorious hodge-podge of leftovers, but you can use almost any meats and vegetables you like, provided the proportions and texture of the ingredients are much the same; avoid watery vegetables, for instance. Good substitutes are cubed raw aubergine or canned butter beans for sweetbread, and green beans for asparagus tips. Strips of turkey drumstick meat can replace pigeon breasts.

FOR THE PASTE:
6oz/150g raw white meat (veal,
   chicken, turkey or rabbit)
5oz/125g dripping or poultry fat
   (scant 3/4 cup)
1/2 tsp each ground mace, grated
   nutmeg and lemon rind
   (3/4 tsp each)
salt and white pepper
1 tsp each chopped parsley and
   dried thyme (1 1/4 tsp each)
1 large egg, beaten
8oz/200g fresh white breadcrumbs,
   or as needed (4 cups)

FOR THE FILLING:
1 tbsp flour (1 1/4 tbsp)

4 thin rashers streaky bacon, diced
   (4 strips)
4 cooked pigeon breasts or pieces of
   brown turkey meat about
   1–1 1/2oz/25–35g each
2oz/50g cooked lamb's sweetbread,
   chopped
3oz/75g green asparagus tips or sliced
   green beans, fresh or canned
3oz/75g mushrooms, chopped
2 hard-boiled eggs, yolks crumbled
5oz/125g cooked pork shoulder or
   roast beef, thinly sliced and cut in
   small squares
1 egg, beaten with a few drops of
   water

Make the paste first. Mince and pound the raw meat and fat together until smooth and pasty, or reduce to paste in a food processor. Mix in the spices, lemon rind, seasoning, herbs and egg, and enough breadcrumbs to make a firm dough-like paste. Grease a 7½–8in/ 180–200mm shallow baking dish or pie plate. Press about half the paste all over the base and sides as lining.

[59]

To fill, scatter half the flour over the base, then the diced bacon. Lay the pigeon breasts, well separated, on the bacon. Use the sweetbread, asparagus tips, mushrooms and crumbled egg yolk to fill the spaces between the pigeon breasts and to cover them. Place the squares of meat on top; the surface should be level and even. Scatter the remaining flour over the meat. Pat out the remaining paste to fit the dish; lay it on top and seal the edges. Pat smooth and glaze with the beaten egg.

Bake at 350°F (180°C), Gas 4 for about 40 minutes until the paste is cooked through and golden brown. Serve with gravy, redcurrant jelly and a green vegetable.

THE HARE-RABBIT.

RABBIT AND OTHER SMALL GAME

—◆◇◆—

Traditional peasants' hedgerow fare, the close-packed low-fat meat of the wild rabbit has excellent food value. If you don't like its slightly musty flavour, skin a home-shot rabbit as soon as it is brought in. Another 'cleanser' is to wipe rabbit meat with a cloth dipped in vinegar-sharpened water before cooking it. Farmed frozen rabbit, although not strictly game, is one of the best-value solid meats the town-dweller can buy. Easily thawed, it is quick and simple to cook and picks up any traditional spicing. Try it with one of the home-made pickles or condiments in Chapter 10 instead of the usual gooseberry or mustard sauce.

Most boneless rabbit meat comes from farmed rabbit specially bred for the table, so it is of course free of any taint of myxomatosis. This 'block rabbit', farmed rabbit joints and whole rabbits can be cooked exactly like chicken. Wild rabbit meat is darker and more sinewy, as well as more gamey. Paunch a wild rabbit as soon as it is killed, then hang it for a few days. Cook it either like chicken or in one of the milder ways of cooking hare. Remember that, on any rabbit, the saddle and hind legs are the fleshiest parts, the forelegs being used mostly for stock. Wild rabbits which have fed on clover or herby land are said to have better-flavoured and firmer flesh than grass-fed ones. For tender flesh, choose a young doe if possible. A young rabbit has flexible joints and smooth claws. Its jaw yields when pressed and its ears tear easily.

RABBIT LAYERS *(Serves 4)*
Sweet corn is not easy to grow and ripen in summers with little sun, and bought cobs are too old and tough to scrape. This is therefore one of the vegetables which it is sensible to buy canned or frozen.

12oz/300g cooked boneless rabbit meat	*7oz/198g can whole-kernel sweetcorn, drained*
1 tbsp corn oil (1¼ tbsp)	*2oz/50g fresh white breadcrumbs*
1 tbsp cornflour (1¼ tbsp cornstarch)	*(1 cup)*
½pt/250ml milk (1¼ cups)	*1 tomato, sliced*
salt and pepper	*sprig of parsley*

Cut the rabbit meat into 1in/2.5cm pieces, and put them into a deep oven-to-table casserole. Heat the oil in a small saucepan. Gradually sprinkle in the cornflour (cornstarch) and cook for 1 minute, stirring. Then, still stirring, slowly add the milk, salt and pepper. Bring to the boil, and pour the mixture over the rabbit meat. Cover with sweetcorn, and sprinkle the breadcrumbs over it.

Bake at 350°F (180°C), Gas 4 for 20–30 minutes. If you wish, raise the heat to 450°F (230°C), Gas 8 for a few moments to gild the top. Garnish with tomato slices and parsley before serving.

CURRIED RABBIT *(Serves 4)*
Although a curry mixture should be simmered for hours to blend the specially chosen flavours, a western-type curry-powder dish can make a welcome change, while not pretending to be subtle.

2 tbsp corn oil (2½ tbsp)	*3 tsp cornflour (4 tsp cornstarch)*
4 rabbit leg joints, thawed if frozen	*½ tsp salt (¾ tsp)*
parsley sprigs, to garnish	*2 tbsp tomato paste (2½ tbsp)*
	1pt/500ml chicken stock (2½ cups)
SAUCE:	*1 large cooking apple*
1 tbsp curry powder (1¼ tbsp)	

Heat the oil in a shallow oven-to-table baking dish. Add the rabbit and cover with foil. Bake at 350°F (180°C), Gas 4 for 45 minutes.

Mix the curry powder, cornflour (cornstarch) salt and tomato paste in a saucepan. Gradually stir in the stock. Still stirring, bring to the boil and simmer for 1–2 minutes. Leave to infuse over the lowest possible heat while you core and peel the apple and cut it into ½in/ 1cm pieces. Stir the apple into the curry sauce, then pour the mixture over the rabbit.

Cover again, and return to the oven for 15–20 minutes until the rabbit is tender. Garnish with parsley just before serving.

STIFADO (Serves 4–6)
Rabbit was the original meat used for this traditional Greek stew, although other meats can be used. You can add to or adapt the other ingredients below too. In Greece the dish is stewed, but baking it saves pot-watching.

4 good-sized rabbit joints, thawed
 if frozen, 7–8oz/175–200g each
2fl oz/50ml olive oil (¼ cup)
1lb/450g small onions, quartered
1–2 cloves garlic, squeezed over onion
4–6 whole cloves, 1in/2.5cm piece
 cinnamon stick and 2–3 parsley
 sprigs tied in a cloth

⅓pt/150ml tomato sauce or ready-
 to-serve soup (¾ cup)
⅓pt/165ml white wine (¾ cup)
salt and pepper
6–8 vine or spinach leaves

Pat the rabbit joints dry. Heat the oil in a deep flameproof casserole, and brown them well. Remove and put in the onions and garlic. Fry until well browned, stirring occasionally. Off the heat, replace the rabbit joints on the onions; then add all the other ingredients in order, ending with a layer of leaves.

Bake, uncovered, at 300°F (150°C), Gas 2 for 2½ hours or until the rabbit is very tender and the sauce is well reduced. Check the liquid occasionally, but don't add extra water unless the sauce looks like drying out. Remove the leaves and the herb bundle.

The dish is better if made ahead, left overnight, then reheated. Serve it with dry boiled rice, but no other vegetables.

Note: More people than you may think, grow vines as ornamental climbing shrubs in their gardens. The local garden centre, for instance, might give you a few leaves to tenderise the meat in summer. In winter — and stifado is perhaps best as a cheap, tasty cold-weather dish — you could use tender cabbage leaves.

4

DAIRY FOODS
TO BEST ADVANTAGE

England has a long dairying tradition, going back to the time when her spreading forests gave way to pastures, and the rough common land became part of the private estates of great noblemen and gentleman farmers. Their sons made the eighteenth century a 'golden age' of butter and cheese, and these two dairy foods became an English habit. Our potted meats for instance (Chapter 6) are traditionally sealed with butter instead of pork or goose fat as in France, and Englishmen still prefer their own unique hard cheeses to any others — understandably, for Cheddar and Stilton are famed world-wide. In the past, most English cream went for butter-making, so English cooks have used rather less of it, as such, than most European cooks; and Britain's large supply of good roasting meat, especially beef, since Stuart times has resulted in eggs being less relied on as main-dish food except in 'the English breakfast'.

With the present cost of meat, however, we need to make the best use of cheese and eggs as main-meal foods, and to get the best value out of the fine flavour of butter. Cream is delicious, but an expensive luxury — there are dozens of ways of making interesting and subtle dishes without it which are better for our health, our pockets and our figures; so I am not focussing on it.

English hard cheese contains, pound for pound, as much protein

[63]

as prime raw beef, and is one of our finest food sources of calcium. Its vitamin A, B_2 and D are also valuable. In fact if eaten with bread (for carbohydrate) and a tomato (for vitamin C, salts and minerals), cheese makes a well-nigh perfectly balanced meal.

It has other advantages. Properly wrapped in foil (not clingfilm), first-grade English or Swiss hard cheese keeps much longer than meat in the refrigerator or larder, and even if a second-grade hard cheese deteriorates by sweating or drying out, it does not become harmful: surface mould can be scraped off, and the cheese can then be used for cooking. Only low-quality cheese or opened, vacuum-packed mild cheese may turn rancid and taste bitter. Cheese is an ideal, easily cut and chewed standby food for elderly people who do not shop often or who are forgetful about the food in their re-frigerator. It should only be refrigerated, not frozen, although a compact bag of frozen grated cheese for cooking is a useful way to package leftover scraps.

Cheese is only indigestible if it is badly cooked. If cooked alone using high heat or for too long, the fat in it runs off, leaving its pro-tein granules, mostly casein, unprotected; they toughen, and the cheese goes ropy. You should cook any cheese gently over low heat, for as short a time as possible, if you use it alone; to make a grilled cheese topping or to use it in a slowly cooked dish, mix it with some other food such as breadcrumbs, crumbled bacon or the roux and liquid of a sauce. Then you need have no qualms about its digestibil-ity, even for old people or the very young.

Egg yolks are high in cholesterol and are fatty — 33% fat, 17% protein and 50% water. People on low-cholesterol or low-fat diets should obviously avoid eggs, both as meals in themselves and hid-den in sauces, cakes and so on. For anyone else, from babies to old people, eggs are an excellent, protein-rich food. They contain iron and vitamins A and D. They keep well on the shelf or (if you must) in the least cold part of the refrigerator; they should be at room temperature when used. Like cheese they are only indigestible if overcooked; then they toughen or curdle.

Try to use very fresh eggs for boiling and poaching. A really fresh egg has a viscous white which holds the yolk in the middle of the shell; a chilled or stale egg usually has a watery white so that the yolk drops through it and lies on the inside of the shell: if you boil or hard-boil the egg, you find a solid mass of white at one end, and the yolk at the other — annoying if you want to stuff it. You can't poach stale eggs properly either: the watery white floats away in strands

[64]

from the yolk in the poaching liquid, instead of being easy to fold round it. Using an egg-poacher, which is really a form of coddling, never gives you a properly enclosed poached (or coddled) egg; it only provides a glazed yolk half-covered by solid rubbery white, low on flavour and digestibility.

Eggs are cheaper in summer than winter, but it's easy to use them too often if you want light meals in hot weather: they are richer than they seem. If you want to serve hard-boiled-egg salads and other egg dishes often, cut down on using eggs in cakes, stuffings and sauces; there are lots of alternatives, such as making crumb cakes, using a grain paste or puréed pulses for 'binding' stuffings and other mixtures, and serving thin salad dressings rather than mayonnaise. Use your eggs whole or in dishes such as soufflés which can't be made without them (and in which they go a long way).

Butter, being the concentrated rich fat of cream, is both expensive and hard on your digestion if you eat too much of it. It is wise, therefore, to keep it (like eggs) for dishes in which its special flavour can be tasted and appreciated to the full. Don't use butter for frying, for instance: it is not, actually, a very good frying medium, as its water content makes it spit, and it both burns and cools quickly, so the fried food can be bitter or soggy. Don't use it for cake-making when other flavours will mask its taste, or in strongly flavoured

[65]

sandwiches if sieved soft cheese will do equally well. *Do* use a dab on steamed or lightly boiled vegetables when you will taste all its goodness. *Do* use it, too, for making savoury butters and for 'potting'; piped lines of a smooth savoury butter on cold meats, for instance, give you a glamorous-looking dish and the full rich flavour of the butter while using very little of it indeed. A potted meat under a thin golden coat of clarified butter looks and tastes luxurious.

STILTON CHEESE.

CHEESE DISHES

BACON AND CHEESE WELL *(Serves 4–6)*
This deep cheese-and-bacon pie is ideal for winter health. Its colourful mixed vegetables are all short-cooked and with the cream, eggs and hard cheese supply almost all the nutrients anyone needs. Made with 4 eggs, the custard is sturdy and sustaining, made with 3 it is delicate enough to be a dinner-party dish.

8oz/200g short crust pastry
butter for greasing
4oz/100g Swiss Gruyère cheese
(scant 1 cup)
4oz/100g streaky bacon rashers
without rind (4 strips)
1/2 medium onion, about 2oz/50g
1 medium leek, about 3oz/75g
1 small carrot, about 3oz/75g

1 medium tomato, about 3oz/75g
4 asparagus stems, frozen or canned
1/2pt/250ml milk (1 1/4 cups)
1/4pt/125ml double cream (1/2 cup
+ 2 tbsp heavy cream)
3 or 4 eggs
salt and pepper
pinch of grated nutmeg

Roll out the pastry and use it to line a greased 7in/175mm loose-bottomed cake tin. Chill while preparing the other ingredients.

Cut the cheese into very small dice, and the bacon into small strips or shreds. Slice the onion and leek into fine rings, and grate the carrot coarsely. Split and seed the tomato, and chop the flesh roughly. If you use frozen asparagus, take 4 stems out of a frozen packet to thaw and return the rest to storage. Drain canned asparagus.

[66]

Put the bacon in a medium saucepan, and stir over gentle heat until the fat runs. Add all the vegetables and stir for 3 minutes until well coated with fat and slightly softened. Leave to cool while you mix the milk and cream in a large jug, and beat in the eggs.

Scatter the cheese cubes over the bottom of the pastry in the tin. Turn in the slightly cooled bacon and vegetables, season the mixture well, and spread it evenly in the tin. Pour the egg and milk mixture over it. Bake at 350°F (180°C), Gas 4 for 1¼ hours. Remove from the tin, slide the 'well' onto a serving plate, and serve hot; or let it cool in the tin for serving cold.

Note: Do not freeze this pie.

BAKED PLOUGHMAN'S BRUNCH *(Serves 6)*
Hearty fare for outdoor workers is just as good for active teenagers, or for informal party eating at any age. Cheese makes a little meat go a long way.

1 round granary loaf (about
  1lb 2oz/525g)
2oz/50g butter or margarine
  (¼ cup)
4oz/100g ham sausage
  (½ cup)
6oz/150g mild hard cheese, finely
  grated (1½ cups)
4oz/100g curd cheese, home-made or
  bought (½ cup)
1 tbsp drained gherkins, chopped
  (1¼ tbsp)
salt and pepper
chopped parsley

GHERKINS.

Cut the loaf in half horizontally. Turn the top half cut-side up. Cut each half into 6 wedges, cutting down to the crust but not right through. Spread with the butter. Put, cut-side up, on a lightly greased baking sheet, and place under the grill until lightly toasted.

Shred the ham sausage and mix with all the remaining ingredients. Spread on the toasted bread, pressing a little down between the wedges. Put in the oven at 400°F (200°C), Gas 6 for 12 minutes, until bubbling. Sprinkle with parsley and serve hot for brunch, TV supper or an informal party.

[67]

GLOUCESTER CASSEROLE *(Serves 6)*

Another way to make cheese a satisfying main meal, with warming everyday vegetables.

1³/4lb/800g potatoes
2 tbsp dried mixed herbs (2¹/2 tbsp)
6oz/150g Double Gloucester cheese
7¹/2oz/213g rindless back bacon rashers (strips)

2oz/50g butter (¹/4 cup)
2oz/50g flour (¹/2 cup)
1pt/500ml skimmed milk (2¹/2 cups)
6oz/150g onion, chopped (1 cup)
salt and pepper

Peel the potatoes and slice them thinly. Sprinkle with the herbs. Grate the cheese. Cut the bacon rashers in half.

Melt the butter in a fair-sized pan, stir in the flour and cook together, stirring, for 2 minutes, without colouring. Gradually stir in the skimmed milk to make a smooth sauce. Bring to the boil, and stir for 3 minutes over low heat, until very thick. Take off the heat, and mix in the onion and 4oz/100g (1 cup) of the cheese. Season well.

Grease lightly a 3pt/1.7 litre (2qt) heavy oven-to-table casserole. Fill it with alternate layers of potato, bacon and sauce, ending with a layer of sauce. Sprinkle all over with the remaining cheese.

Cover the casserole closely with foil or a lid and bake at 375°F (190°C), Gas 5 for 1¹/2 hours. Uncover for the last 6–8 minutes. Serve from the casserole.

BAKED CHEESE GNOCCHI *(Serves 4 main helpings)*

3oz/75g Swiss Gruyère cheese, grated (²/3 cup)
3oz/75g grated Parmesan cheese (²/3 cup)
2oz/50g butter (¹/4 cup)

1pt/500ml milk (2¹/2 cups)
4oz/100g semolina (²/3 cup)
salt and white pepper
¹/2 tsp grated nutmeg (³/4 tsp)
2 eggs

Mix the Swiss cheese with the Parmesan. Use ¹/2oz/15g (1 tbsp) of the butter to grease a 10in x 12in/250mm x 300mm baking tin.

Bring the milk to the boil in a saucepan, and stir in the semolina, salt, pepper and nutmeg. Stir over gentle heat until the mixture is very thick. Take off the heat. Beat the eggs until liquid, then stir them gradually but very thoroughly into the semolina, with 5oz/125g (1¹/4 cups) of the mixed cheeses. Spread the mixture in a ¹/2in/1cm layer in the tin, and leave to get quite cold.

Cut the mixture into 1in/2.5cm squares. Grease a shallow, oven-to-table dish with another ¹/2oz/15g (1 tbsp) of the butter and lay the gnocchi in it in a single layer. Sprinkle them with the remaining cheese and dot with the rest of the butter. Bake for 5–6 minutes at 400°F (200°C), Gas 6, until the cheese topping bubbles and browns slightly. Serve from the dish.

Good with Home-made Tomato Sauce (page 25) or with hot Ratatouille (page 139).

CHEESE GLASS.

RAREBITS

A rarebit used to be simply a small dish of melted cheese, often cooked with beer or wine and called 'stewed' or 'roast' cheese; it was poured over wine-soaked toast or served with dry toast fingers. These days the toast is spread with a thick, pasty sauce mixture, and is lightly grilled like a toasted open sandwich. The main ingredient is still usually cheese, but white sauce or other foods are often added to give the rarebit bulk, flavour or character.

Quickly made, a rarebit is most often used for a snack meal, or for high tea or supper; but it can be quite substantial enough for a main-course dish.

Surround a main-course rarebit with crisp, freshly cooked vegetables such as sliced green beans, and serve it quickly before it has any chance to cool and become leathery.

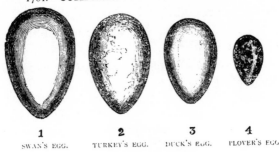

1	2	3	4
SWAN'S EGG.	TURKEY'S EGG.	DUCK'S EGG.	PLOVER'S EGG.

EGG DISHES

—◆◆—

CREAMY CAULIFLOWER 'CAKE' *(Serves 6)*

Quick to prepare, this substantial omelette makes a good Sunday night supper. Serve it very hot, straight from the pan.

1/2 small head cauliflower
1oz/25g walnut pieces, chopped
  (1/4 cup)
1 small onion
1oz/25g butter (2 tbsp)
8oz/200g high bran or wheatgerm
  brown bread without crusts

salt and pepper
pinch of grated nutmeg
3 eggs
4 tbsp single cream (5 tbsp light
  cream)
3 1/2 fl oz/90ml milk (scant 1/2 cup)

Break the cauliflower into sprigs, and cook in water until just tender. Drain, and mix with the nuts.

Chop the onion. Melt the butter in an 8in/200mm omelette pan or deep frying pan (skillet), and fry the onion gently until just browned. Cut the bread into 3/4in/2cm cubes, and add the fried onion, leaving the fat in the pan. Season the bread cubes and onion with the salt, pepper and nutmeg.

Pack half the bread and onion into the pan, evenly. Cover with with the cauliflower and nuts, then with the rest of the bread cubes. Beat the eggs with the cream and milk until well blended. Pour half the liquid into the pan. Cover and cook over medium heat, shaking the pan, until the 'cake' is golden brown underneath.

Put a large plate upside-down on the pan, and turn the pan and plate over so that the omelette is on the plate, browned side up. Pour the rest of the liquid into the pan, and slide in the omelette, still browned side up. Replace on the heat, cover and cook as before until golden brown underneath. Serve immediately.

TURNIP SOUFFLÉ *(Serves 4)*

Make the most of a pedestrian vegetable by using it for a subtly flavoured soufflé.

*about 8oz/200g young turnips
   (see method)*
butter for greasing and frying
2oz/50g butter for soufflé (¼ cup)
2 tbsp grated onion (2½ tbsp)
3 tbsp white flour (4 tbsp)
*4fl oz/100ml vegetable stock or
   water in which the turnips
   have cooked (½ cup)*

4fl oz/100ml milk (½ cup)
2 tbsp chopped parsley (2½ tbsp)
pinch of ground coriander
salt and pepper
4 eggs

Cook, peel and purée the turnips. The quantity of purée should be 6oz/150g. Grease the inside of a 7in/175mm soufflé dish with butter and use about 2 tsp (2½ tsp) more butter to 'sweat' the grated onion until soft but not coloured. Mix the onion with the turnip purée.

Melt the 2oz/50g (¼ cup) butter in a fairly large saucepan over low heat, and stir in the flour. Continue stirring for 3 minutes without letting the flour colour. Mix the stock or water and the milk together, and add the liquid gradually to the roux, stirring all the time. Continue stirring until thick and well blended. Simmer gently for 3 minutes. Then stir in, smoothly, the turnip purée, parsley, coriander and seasoning. Take off the heat and cool for 5 minutes. While cooling, separate the eggs and beat the yolks lightly. Mix them into the cooled purée.

Whisk the whites until stiff with a pinch of extra salt. Stir one spoonful into the purée, then fold in the rest. Turn the purée very gently into the soufflé dish. Bake for 25–30 minutes at 375°F (190°C), Gas 5. Serve immediately.

Note: Use Cornish turnips (swedes) for a beautifully coloured and flavoured soufflé. Parsnips also make an attractive soufflé; use grated nutmeg instead of coriander.

TURNIPS.

EGG BALLS *(makes about 20)*
A good nineteenth-century way to make a showy use of eggs without extra fat. Scatter the small egg 'marbles' on a salad to make it a main dish, or use them to garnish consommé by putting a couple in each bowl. They could hardly be quicker or easier to make.

6 medium (size 3) eggs
1 egg yolk
½ tsp flour (¾ tsp)

salt
pinch of cayenne pepper

Hard-boil the 6 eggs for 10 minutes. At once, put in cold water and cool. When cold, remove the yolks (the whites can be chopped and used to garnish a pâté, a rice dish such as kedgeree or a chef's salad).

With the back of a spoon, work the hard-boiled yolks with the raw yolk, flour and seasonings until pasty. Roll into small 'marbles'. Bring a pan of salted water to simmering point, put in the 'marbles' and simmer for 2 minutes without shaking the pan. Drain in a nylon sieve, and use as you wish.

SPINACH PUDDING *(Serves 4)*
A savoury spinach soufflé is a delicious 'classic'; this intriguing old sweet pudding is equally light and delicate, but more unusual today.

about 8oz/200g chopped cooked
spinach from 1½–2lb raw
spinach (700–900g)
3 eggs
pinch of table salt
2oz/50g caster sugar
¼ pt/125ml single cream (½ cup
+ 2 tbsp)

1oz/25g fine dried white
breadcrumbs (⅓ cup)
pinch of grated nutmeg
2fl oz/50ml melted butter (¼ cup)
1oz/25g melted butter for greasing
(2 tbsp)
single cream (light cream)

Drain the spinach very thoroughly and pound it to a purée (or use a food processor). Beat together the eggs, salt and sugar until liquid and frothy. Beat in the cream, crumbs and nutmeg. Stir well, then mix with the spinach purée and melted butter.

Put a thick cloth in the bottom of a large pan of water; bring the water to simmering point. Grease a 2pt/1.1 litre pudding basin with melted butter; turn the mixture lightly into it and cover tightly. Lower the basin into the water, which should reach half way up its sides. Simmer for 45 minutes–1 hour, until the pudding is firm in the middle. Remove the basin from the pan, and let the pudding stand at room temperature for 10 minutes. Turn out onto a warmed dish. Serve with cream.

[72]

MAKING THE MOST OF BUTTER

——◆◇◆——

Savoury butters for spreads and garnishing are traditionally English, and being uncooked demand the pure creamy taste of butter itself to bring out their full flavour; no substitute will really do. Use slightly salted butter.

BUTTER-DISH.

Use pure unsalted butter for butter icings and buttercreams, which are also uncooked. A discerning palate can pick up the hint of any other fat or oil. Although a trace of salt deepens the flavour of any sweet butter confection, it *must* be made basically with *un*salted butter. This, too, is traditional. From medieval times until the late nineteenth century heavily salted butter was the poor man's staple savoury spread, but unsalted butter, which did not keep well, was reserved for making luxuries for the rich man's table; and butter icings (like 'hard' and other butter sauces) are certainly luxuries!

To make the most of them economically, use the same trick as when garnishing a savoury dish. Put the softened sweet buttercream into a forcing bag with a small pipe nozzle; then, instead of covering the whole top of a cake with icing, pipe a fanciful pattern of lines and rosettes on it. It can look even more effective and does not mask the cake's own flavour or overload people's stomachs — and it is certainly cheaper.

For another good use of butter, see the recipes for potted meats (pages 103–5). Remember, too, that a little melted butter in a sauce boat is the quickest, easiest sauce you can make for plainly cooked poultry, game birds or vegetables, and compensates for any extra cost by using no labour or fuel.

A savoury butter, flavoured with a salty or pickled ingredient or hard cheese, is a way of using butter which should keep well for 2 weeks in the refrigerator. Butters containing fresh meat or fish, herbs or green leaves should be used within a week; after that, the flavour may deteriorate, and unsalted or lightly salted butter may begin to turn rancid. See Chapter 8 for interesting herb butters.

[73]

ANCHOVY BUTTER *(Makes 4oz/100g [¹/₂ cup])*

8 anchovy fillets, drained
4oz/100g unsalted butter, softened (¹/₂ cup)

Pound or grind the fillets to a paste and mash into the butter. Press into a small pot, tapping on the table once or twice while filling to knock out air spaces. Level and smooth the surface, then cover with clingfilm and refrigerate until needed. Use within 2 weeks.

For a smooth anchovy butter for piping, use a few drops of anchovy essence instead of fillets, and add a drop or two of bright red food colouring (not cochineal) to tint the butter a light orangy pink.

DERBYSHIRE BUTTER *(Makes about 8oz/200g [1 cup])*
A very old 'butter' which makes a good sandwich spread.

4oz/100g minced cooked chicken
  or rabbit (¹/₂ cup)
6 anchovy fillets
6oz/150g butter, softened (³/₄ cup)

¹/₂ tsp mild French mustard (³/₄ tsp)
a few grains of cayenne pepper
grated Parmesan cheese for sprinkling

Pound meat and anchovies together until like a coarse pâté. Mix in all the other ingredients in order, except the cheese. Alternatively, put all the ingredients in a food processor and process until thoroughly mixed.

Serve on canapés for cocktail snacks, or use as a savoury tartlet filling, in both cases sprinkled with the cheese. For sandwiches, sprinkle with cheese before closing the sandwich.

MRS SMITH'S ALMOND BUTTER *(Makes about 8oz/200g [1 cup])*
The eighteenth-century author recommended sieving this concoction into a dish to serve as a 'spoon sweet'. But it is rich, and is better used as a cake filling today.

3oz/75g unsalted butter (¹/₃ cup)
3oz/75g ground almonds (¹/₃ cup)
1 tbsp triple-strength rose water
  (1¹/₄ tbsp)

2–3 drops rose or almond essence
2–3 drops vanilla essence
1¹/₂oz/35g caster sugar (¹/₄ cup)

Soften the butter. Put the almonds, liquids and butter into a bowl and beat thoroughly until fully blended. Beat in the sugar likewise. Taste and add more flavouring if required, then beat again, very thoroughly to obtain as smooth a cream as possible. Alternatively blend in a food processor.

Fill into small pots or cream cartons, in the same way as for Anchovy Butter (opposite). Cover, and chill if not for immediate use. It keeps excellently.

MRS BEETON'S FAIRY BUTTER, 1860 *(Makes about 6oz/150g [³/4 cup])*
A Victorian 'butter' this time. This one was popular in the previous century too: Mrs Raffald gives a recipe for it.

2 hard-boiled egg yolks	*1oz/25g icing sugar (¹/4 cup)*
pinch of salt	*2 tsp strained orange juice (2¹/2 tsp)*
4oz/100g unsalted butter, softened	*2 tsp finely grated orange rind*
(¹/2 cup)	*(2¹/2 tsp) (optional)*

Sieve the egg yolks and salt, then beat in the butter, sugar, liquid and rind alternately until they form a smooth pasty mass. Alternatively, process all the ingredients in a food processor or blender. (Don't use orange rind if you want to pipe the butter.)

Pack into small pots in the same way as Anchovy Butter (opposite). Cover and chill until required. The butter keeps for at least 2 weeks under refrigeration.

You can use this butter as a cake filling or for decorating, like any other sweet butter: or you can serve it in the old way by passing it through a coarse-meshed wire sieve so that it falls in strands like vermicelli. Victorian hostesses would offer it for spreading on sweet breads or biscuits at tea-time, or instead of a sauce or cream with certain dinner-time puddings and desserts.

GUARD SAUCE *(Serves 4)*
This is an old name, and an old recipe, for brandy butter. I have changed it by using ground almonds instead of bitter almonds for safety's sake (see note) and by using only a quarter of the original quantity of brandy. Our forebears liked their flavours and their liquor strong.

4oz/100g slightly salted butter	*2oz/50g caster sugar (scant ¹/2 cup)*
(¹/2 cup)	*2fl oz/50ml brandy (¹/4cup)*
1 oz/25g ground almonds (¹/4 cup)	

Soften the butter — by putting it in a bowl standing in a pan of warm (not hot) water if the weather is cold. Beat it, using a rotary or electric beater, until very creamy and light. Slowly beat in the other

[75]

ingredients in order, trickling in the brandy last, carefully, to prevent the mixture separating.

Serve the sauce as it is, like thick whipped cream, or chill it in a shallow bowl — in which case it should be very light and cold, almost like a mousse, when served.

Note: Bitter almonds have a more 'almondy' flavour than sweet almonds, but they contain prussic acid. It is so easy to use them instead of sweet almonds by mistake that I never keep them on my shelf.

BASIC BUTTER ICING *(Makes enough to cover one 7¹/₂in/19cm cake)*

1oz/25g butter (2 tbsp)	*2–3 tbsp hot single cream (3–4 tbsp*
pinch of salt	*light cream)*
8oz/200g sifted icing sugar (2¹/₄	*flavouring, eg ¹/₂ tsp vanilla essence*
cups confectioner's sugar)	*(³/₄ tsp)*

Beat together the butter, salt and sugar until light and fluffy. Still beating, gradually trickle in the cream and flavouring. Continue beating until the icing is thick enough to spread. Use a hot wet knife for spreading — the icing stiffens quickly.

Variation:
For Lemon Butter Icing, flavour with ½ tbsp (¾ tbsp) strained lemon juice.

[76]

BASIC BUTTERCREAM *(Makes about 12oz/300g [1¹/2 cups])*
Use this basic buttercream for fillings.

4oz/100g butter, softened
  (¹/2 cup)
8oz/200g sifted icing sugar (scant
  2 cups confectioner's sugar)

¹/2–1 tbsp hot single cream
  (³/4–1¹/4 tbsp light cream)
¹/2 tsp vanilla essence or other
  flavouring to taste (³/4 tsp)

Make like Basic Butter Icing (previous recipe). Chill if necessary before use.

5

MAKING YOUR OWN BREADS

—◆◇—

Making bread is a deeply satisfying craft, perhaps because bread is a basic food, satisfying in itself. Yeast, too, behaves differently from any other ingredient, being alive; so although it is easier to handle than, say, eggs, one always has a momentary feeling of triumph when the liquid froths, or one feels the dough suddenly 'come' under the kneading.

Home-made bread can give you fresh, moist or dryish bread for crumbs whenever you need them. You can add an almost infinite number of different nutrients, including pulses or straight protein foods such as cheese or bacon; you can make savoury or sweet breads, and vary their fibre content as you please. You can use mixed flours, so that you can keep several kinds in stock for other cooking, knowing they will be used well within their shelf-life.

Yeast is one of the most good-tempered products we use. In fact, yeast bread should really be called a 'convenience' food. You can raise and make it in one session, or put it in the refrigerator before or after raising it. It will rise in any fairly warm place, reasonably free from draughts. Often, the easiest way is simply to leave it at room temperature in a modern centrally heated or reasonably warm kitchen overnight. Given dried yeast and a refrigerator for extra-slow rising, bread can be made within the time schedules of most office workers, and even more easily than casseroles and stews.

If you want bread quickly, baking-powder or 'quick' breads are, of course, the ideal answer. You can vary them in the same way as yeast breads, and few take longer than an hour to bake; most are much quicker. Semi-sweet breads can save you making cakes too; in fact many Americans call semi-sweet breads 'coffee cakes'.

Then there are the small breakfast and tea 'breads'. Rolls, scones, buns and drop scones serve dozens of purposes. You can use them instead of sandwiches in packed meals, instead of cakes with jam and perhaps cream, or even as the basis of desserts.

In traditional chowders, cobblers and filled fried-bread cases bread is used as an essential part of a main dish; and there's nothing wrong with toasted cheese or open sandwiches as a TV or tray meal. Making 'quick' or tea breads is a good way of using up leftovers too; even the end of a packet of porridge oats, dry muesli or cornflakes can be a useful ingredient.

So this is a long chapter, showing you just some of the many variations in flavour you can achieve; adapt them and use them as a basis for variations of your own. For instance, give your breads different toppings: pumpkin or poppy seeds, crushed nuts or cornflakes, bacon or crispbread crumbs all make good 'crusts'. As for the contents, the choice of flavourings and additions is almost endless.

Most of the recipes here use wholewheat or mixed flour; if you cannot get the suggested flour, it will seldom matter if you substitute one like it. For instance, instead of using an 85 per cent extraction flour, use half wholemeal and half white flour, with perhaps a teaspoon of natural wheat bran. If you cannot get fine oatmeal, make your own by grinding medium oatmeal in a food processor or blender. A few sample fresh-food additions (seeds, grated apple, and so on) are included, but you can substitute others, and you will create interesting textures and tastes by doing so. As a rule, you can adapt bread doughs, provided the moisture content and weight of any substitutes are about the same as in the original recipe.

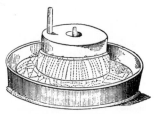

QUERN, OR GRINDING-MILL.

[79]

Some of the breads below are whole loaves. Others are small buns, scones or snack breads. Some, especially the older ones, are sweetish, close to cakes.

Cakes, in fact, began as bits of bread dough enriched with fat, dried fruit and spices as a treat; and up to Victorian times and after, plain cakes were still raised with yeast like breads. On page 174, you will find an example of this plain, satisfying kind of cake which we have (wrongly) almost forgotten.

Making the dough
You can use either fresh or dried yeast in any recipe, but use only half as much dried yeast. The general method is to blend fresh yeast to a cream with a little liquid. Put a good pinch of sugar or a few drops of honey in the liquid first if you use dried yeast. Then, instead of creaming, sprinkle the dried yeast onto the sweetened liquid and leave it until it forms a thick soft frothy mass on top; it takes 10–15 minutes, depending on the temperature of the liquid. Then add it to your recipe in the same way as fresh yeast.

When you have mixed the yeast liquid into the drier ingredients, you will have to knead the dough to break down the starch granules. Shape it into a cushion, and 'tread' it with your knuckles or the heel of your hand, pressing down from the centre outwards and turning the cushion so that you attack a different piece of dough each time.

Fold the spread-out piece back over itself, to keep the cushion shape. For a little while, the dough will be just an inert lump, and then, in a moment, you will feel it stretch resiliently under your hands; when this happens, we say that the dough has 'come'. You can then mould the dough into the shape your recipe tells you, and leave it to rise.

In most, but not all, recipes, you will knead the risen dough again briefly (this is called 'knocking back') to form it into its final shape, and leave it to rise again or 'prove'.

Storing breads
Most breads freeze perfectly, or can be kept moist for several days in the refrigerator if closely wrapped without air. Moist fruit breads and gingerbreads store very well in an airtight tin. Any wholemeal bread dries out slightly more quickly than white bread, however. Using modern ingredients in centrally heated homes, our storage problem is quite different from that of past cooks. They were more concerned about keeping their bread from going damp and mouldy, and put a cut potato in the bread crock or stored bread and oatcakes in a bin of dry meal to prevent it. We use much less liquid in our breads and cakes than they did, and our homes are drier and warmer.

If by chance a whole or half loaf goes stale before it can be used, there are several ways in which you can put it to good use which you may not think of when the moment strikes and which can be real economy measures (see page 95). Scones, split and filled with a little stewed fruit and thick custard, with another dollop of custard on top, can be served as the well-known American dessert, Fruit Shortcake.

YEAST BREADS AND ROLLS
(including sweet baked goods)

—◆◇—

WHOLEMEAL BREAD AND ROLLS *(Makes two 13oz/350g tin or bun loaves and 10–12 rolls; or 4 small loaves)*

2oz/50g margarine or lard (¹/4 cup)
1oz/25g fresh yeast
¹/4 tsp honey (¹/2 tsp)
1–1¹/2pt/500–850ml warm water
  (2¹/2–3³/4 cups)

2¹/4lb/1kg wholemeal bread flour
¹/2oz/15g salt
margarine or lard for greasing

Vary the quantity of water to suit the flour. The milling, the flour's quality, even the weather may make it need more or less water than usual. If you bake the bread in tins, make the dough slightly damper than for bun loaves or rolls.

Melt the fat and leave to cool. Cream the yeast and honey with a little of the water. Put the flour and salt in a large bowl, and make a hollow in the centre. Tip in the creamed yeast, cooled fat and 1pt/500ml (2¹/2 cups) of the remaining water. Mix in by hand until you have a fairly solid dough. Add most of the remaining water if the dough still seems dry or if you intend to bake all the bread as loaves.

Knead the dough with your knuckles and the heels of your hands. Then either refrigerate it for up to 12 hours before raising it, or put it in a warm place, with a lid on the bowl, for about 2 hours, until almost doubled in bulk.

[82]

Form the risen dough into a more or less square shape on a lightly floured surface. Cut it into 4 equal portions. To make it all into loaves, grease 7½in x 4in/185mm x 100mm (1lb/450g) loaf tins or a baking sheet (for bun loaves). Put one portion into each tin, filling the tins only half full, and pressing the dough well down into the corners. Shape bun loaves into rounds and cut a deep cross in the top of each; not just for looks but to let air and heat penetrate the dough.

Rolls, also cooked on a greased baking sheet, can be any shape you like. A useful one is the 'fanlight', for which you make a flattish round shape like a hamburger, then fold it in half. This allows you to put any 'extra' such as chopped herbs or a scrap of grated cheese on the round before folding it, and it will be baked in.

Leave the loaves and rolls in a warm place for ¾–1 hour. Rolls will rise sooner, but you can leave them with the bread unless it is more convenient to bake them first. The bread is ready when slightly swollen and yielding. Bake either kind of loaf, and the rolls, at 425°F (220°C), Gas 7 for 20 minutes. Remove rolls, and bake loaves at the same temperature for another 10 minutes; then reduce the heat to 325°F (160°C), Gas 3 and bake about 15 minutes longer. The loaves should sound hollow when tapped on the bottom. Cool on a wire rack.

Variations:

1   Form bun loaves into sausage shapes and make 3 diagonal slits in the top of each instead of a cross.

2   Form rolls by making flat rectangles of dough, then roll them up like small Swiss rolls.

3   Make tiny button rolls, the size of button-mushroom caps. Use them as cocktail-hour snacks, split and filled with a savoury filling (pages 113–14).

4   Glaze the loaves or rolls with beaten egg mixed with a few drops of water before baking. Sprinkle with sesame or poppy seeds, crushed wheat or oat flakes or coarse oatmeal.

WHOLEMEAL EGG BREAD OR BRIOCHE ROLLS *(Makes one 6in/150mm 'flowerpot' loaf or 14 rolls)*

2 tsp light muscovado sugar
  (2½ tsp)
4 tbsp warm water (5 tbsp)
1 tbsp dried yeast (1 tbsp)
1lb/450g wholemeal bread flour
  (4 cups)

1 tsp salt (1¼ tsp)
2oz/50g butter or margarine (¼ cup)
3 eggs, beaten
beaten egg to glaze (optional)
butter for greasing

Stir a good pinch of sugar into the water, and sprinkle on the yeast. Leave until frothy. Mix the flour, salt and remaining sugar in a large bowl. Rub or beat in the fat. When crumbly, make a hollow in the middle and pour in the eggs. Tip in the yeast liquid. Stir together to form a dough. Then knead the mixture in the bowl to incorporate all the flour completely and make the dough elastic. When it 'comes', cover the bowl, and leave in a warm place for 45 minutes or until the dough is well risen and puffy.

Grease a brioche tin or charlotte mould about 6in/150mm diameter and 3in/75mm high, or fourteen 2½–3in/60–75mm deep bun tins. Press the dough into the large tin and level the top; or shape into round rolls and put in the bun tins. With a sharp knife-point, cut a circle in the centre top of the loaf about 2in/5cm across, or make small circular slits in the tops of the buns with a ½in/10mm pastry cutter. Cover the loaf or rolls loosely and put in a warm place for about 30 minutes.

Brush lightly with beaten egg if used. Bake at 450°F (230°C), Gas 8 for about 12 minutes in the case of small brioches, 30–40 minutes if making one large loaf. Cover loosely for the last 4–5 minutes if becoming too brown. The bread is done if it sounds hollow when tapped on the bottom. Cool on a wire rack.

In the past, brioche rolls were often used as stuffed cases. The tops were cut off, most of the crumb was removed, and a savoury filling was substituted. The 'caps' were put back and the rolls were warmed in the oven to serve as an entrée or breakfast dish. It is worth doing for a TV supper. Try chicken and chopped mushroom in a thick white sauce, or cooked smoked haddock and puréed canned tomatoes.

HERB BREAD *(Makes one 12oz/300g loaf and 6 rolls)*
Colour picture page 34.

8oz/200g plain white flour (bread flour if possible) (2 cups)
8oz/200g wholewheat flour (2 cups)
1 tsp salt (1¼ tsp)
1 tsp sugar (1¼ tsp)
1 tsp mixed dried herbs (1¼ tsp)
½oz/15g margarine (2 tsp)
½oz/15g fresh yeast or 2 tsp dried yeast (2½ tsp)

½pt/250ml tepid water (1¼ cups)
¼ tsp clear honey (½ tsp)
margarine for greasing

TOPPING:
½oz/15g margarine, melted
¼ tsp mixed dried herbs (½ tsp)

Mix the flours, salt, sugar and the 1 tsp (1¼ tsp) herbs. Rub in the margarine. Blend fresh yeast to a cream with a little of the water and the honey. Sprinkle dried yeast on about half the water mixed with the honey, and leave for 15 minutes. Mix in remaining water. Add to the dry ingredients all at once. Beat well to make a soft dough which leaves the sides of the bowl clean.

Turn onto a lightly floured surface, and knead for 8–10 minutes or until the dough is firm and elastic. Divide it into 2 equal parts. Cut one part into four 3oz/75g pieces and roll each into a ball. Place them in a row in a greased 7½in x 4in/185mm x 100mm (1lb/450g) loaf tin. Brush the tops with melted margarine and sprinkle with herbs. Place in a lightly oiled polythene bag and leave until the dough has risen just above the tin; the time will depend on how warm it is. Shape the rest of the dough into 6 individual rolls; place on a baking sheet and leave until doubled in size.

Bake at 450°F (230°C), Gas 8 for about 30 minutes or 12–15 minutes for rolls, until they sound hollow when tapped underneath.

POTATO BREAD *(Makes two 1lb/450g loaves)*
Flat potato cakes are well known, but this almost sweet, grainy wholewheat bread is quite different. It's a good choice for eating with cheese or pickle as a quick lunch or supper.

4 tsp honey (5 tsp)	*8oz/200g mashed potato (1 cup)*
4 fl oz/100ml lukewarm water	*2½oz/65g semolina (½ cup)*
(½ cup)	*6oz/150g wholewheat flour*
4 tsp dried yeast (5 tsp)	*(1½ cups)*
½ tsp salt (½ tsp)	*8 tsp butter (10 tsp)*
4 tsp vegetable oil (5 tsp)	*margarine for greasing*

Stir the honey into the water in a large mixing bowl, and sprinkle on the yeast. Leave to stand until frothy. Add the salt and oil, then stir in the mashed potato, semolina and 4oz/100g (1 cup) of the flour. Mix thoroughly. Spread in a 2in/5cm layer on floured paper, cover with a cloth and leave to stand for 10 minutes.

Scatter the butter in small dots all over the dough. Fold the dough over it, and knead in the rest of the flour. Continue kneading for 5 minutes, adding a little more flour if needed to make a pliant dough. Grease lightly two 7½in x 4in x 2in/185mm x 100mm x 50mm loaf tins, place half the dough in each, cover and leave for about 30 minutes until doubled in size.

Bake at 375°F (190°C), Gas 5 for 35–40 minutes. The tops should be brown but still soft. Cool on a rack, then slice for serving.

MUSHROOM BREAD *(Makes one 1³/₄lb/800g loaf)*

³/₄oz/20g dried yeast
good ¹/₄pt/130ml warm water
  (³/₄ cup)
4fl oz/100ml milk (¹/₂ cup)
¹/₂oz/15g butter, softened
  (1¹/₂ tbsp)
¹/₂oz/15g sugar (2 tbsp)
good pinch of salt
14oz/375g wholemeal flour
  (3¹/₂ cups)

3¹/₂oz/85g white bread flour
  (³/₄ cup + 2 tbsp)
¹/₂oz/15g natural wheat bran (4 tbsp)
butter for greasing
4oz/100g mushrooms (cup or button)
¹/₂ tbsp dried sliced onions, soaked
  and drained (³/₄ tbsp)
butter for greasing

Sprinkle the yeast on the warm water in a large bowl, and leave until frothy. Scald the milk, and dissolve the butter, sugar and salt in it. Add to the yeast. Mix the two flours together on stout paper, and put 2¹/₂oz/65g (good ¹/₂ cup) aside. Sift the rest into the bowl, return any bran in the sifter to the bowl, and add the ¹/₂oz/15g (4 tbsp) natural bran. Stir the dry ingredients into the yeast mixture with a spoon, then mix with your hands to a firm dough. On a lightly floured surface, knead until elastic and shiny.

Butter the inside of the bowl generously. Turn the dough over in it, to film it with butter. Cover loosely, and leave in a warm place until doubled in bulk.

Chop the mushrooms finely, and mix with the onions. Mix by spoonfuls into the dough. (The mushrooms will make the dough quite sticky.) Sprinkle half the reserved flour on a board, and knead it into the dough. Then knead in enough of the remaining flour to make the dough firm (you may not need it all). Knead 5 minutes longer.

Butter a 2lb/1kg loaf tin. Shape the dough into a rectangle and put it in the tin. Butter the top lightly. Leave in a warm place for 30 minutes.

Bake at 375°F (190°C), Gas 5 for 45 minutes or until the loaf sounds hollow when tapped on the bottom. Cool on a wire rack.

THE MUSHROOM.

[86]

OATMEAL DROP SCONES (Makes 12–14 scones)

Although fried, these yeast-raised girdle scones have the texture and taste of sweet bread, and can be kept for up to 2 days in an airtight tin. Cook them very slowly so that the outside does not harden before the mixture is cooked in the centre.

1/2oz/15g fresh yeast or
  1/4oz/8g dried yeast
1 1/2oz/15g light muscovado sugar
  (1 tbsp)
2 tbsp tepid milk (2 1/2 tbsp)
4oz/100g plain white flour (1 cup)

4oz/100g wholemeal flour (1 cup)
3oz/75g fine oatmeal (3/4 cup)
1/4 tsp salt (1/2 tsp)
1/2pt/250ml cold milk (1 1/4 cups)
1 egg
oil for greasing

Cream fresh yeast with the sugar and tepid milk in a fairly large mixing bowl. Scatter dried yeast on the sweetened liquid and leave until frothy. Mix the white flour, wholemeal flour, oatmeal and salt on a sheet of paper, and tip the mixture into the bowl. Warm the cold milk to tepid, then whisk in the egg, and pour the mixture over the dry goods. Stir all the ingredients together to make a soft-dropping batter. Cover the bowl loosely and leave at room temperature for 30 minutes or until the mixture is thick and spongy.

Heat just enough oil on a girdle or in a large heavy frying pan to film the bottom thinly. With a soup or serving spoon, scoop up spoonfuls of 'sponge' and drop 3 or 4 onto the heated surface; yeast batters are tacky so you may have to scrape the batter off the spoon with a palette knife. Do not flatten the mounds of 'sponge'. Turn down the heat and cook them very gently until lightly browned underneath. Turn over, and cook the other side until no white line of uncooked batter shows in the centre. The scones should be 1/2–2/3in/ 1–1.5cm thick. Transfer each batch to soft kitchen paper when cooked, continuing until all the batter has been used.

Spread the scones with butter and eat at once, while still warm; or cool, and store in an airtight tin for up to 48 hours. Reheat between two plates or wrapped in foil, then split and butter them.

The scones also make a good packed-meal alternative to sandwiches. Use within 24 hours of making, split, buttered and filled with a savoury spread (pages 113–14).

SPICED YEAST BUNS *(makes 18 buns)*

*9fl oz/225ml water (1 cup +
  2 tbsp)*
*3oz/75g light soft brown sugar
  (1/3 cup)*
1 tbsp dried yeast (1 tbsp)
*2oz/50g butter or margarine
  (1/4 cup)*
*1lb/450g plain wholemeal flour or
  85 per cent extraction flour
  (4 cups)*

4 tsp mixed spice (5 tsp)
1 tsp salt (1 1/4 tsp)
1oz/25g sultanas (1 1/2 tbsp)
3oz/75g currants (1/2 cup)
*1oz/25g chopped mixed peel
  (1 1/2 tbsp)*
butter, margarine or oil for greasing
flour for dredging

Heat the water to 110°F/43–44°C. Put about 3fl oz/ 75ml (1/3 cup) of it into a small warm basin, and mix in 1/2 tsp (3/4 tsp) of the sugar. Stir until the sugar is dissolved, sprinkle on the yeast. Whisk it in, and leave it for 15 minutes in a warm place.

Rub the fat into the flour and spice. Put the rest of the sugar and the salt into the remaining water. Blend it with the yeast mixture, then mix the liquids into the dry flour and fat to make a smooth dough. Knead in the fruit, mixing thoroughly. Leave in a warm place for 30 minutes.

Divide the dough into 18 equal-sized pieces and shape into round balls. Place on a warmed, lightly greased and floured baking tray; cover lightly, and leave in a warm place for 40–45 minutes. Bake at 425°F (220°C), Gas 7 for 15–20 minutes until crusty. Cool on a wire rack.

BUNS.

QUICK-LEAVENED BAKED GOODS

—◆◆—

PLAIN BAKING-POWDER BREAD *(Makes two 14oz/375–400g loaves)*

8oz/200g white self-raising flour (2 cups)
8oz/200g wholemeal self-raising flour (2 cups)
1 tsp salt (1¹/₄ tsp)
2oz/50g margarine (¹/₄ cup)
2oz/50g chopped mixed nuts (¹/₂ cup) (optional)

¹/₂pt/250ml milk or milk and water mixed (1¹/₄ cups) (see note)
1 egg, well beaten (optional)
crushed wheat as needed
oil for greasing

Shake both flours and the salt together in a large bowl, and rub in the fat to make fine even crumbs. Add the nuts. Mix in enough milk or milk and water to make a soft dough, adding the egg if used; you will probably need the full ¹/₂pt/250ml (1¹/₄ cups) without the egg.

Turn the mixture onto a surface dusted with wholemeal flour, and knead for 1 minute. Shape the dough into 2 rounds, and make a cross in the top of each. Sprinkle the tops of the loaves with crushed wheat, and place on a lightly greased baking sheet.

Bake the loaves at 400°F (200°C), Gas 6 for 30–40 minutes, until they sound hollow when tapped on the bottom. Cool on a rack.

Note: Substitute up to 2fl oz/50ml (¹/₄ cup) water for milk if you want a really light, plain bread. To glaze, brush the tops of the loaves lightly with extra beaten egg before sprinkling with crushed wheat.

OLD ENGLISH APPLE BREAD *(Makes one 1¼lb/625g loaf)*

Team the goodness of fruit and traditional cider with stone-ground flour to make a health-packed bread.

2oz/50g butter (¼ cup)
12oz/300g self-raising 85 per cent
  extraction flour (3 cups)
  (see note)
½ tsp salt (¾ tsp)
3oz/75g cored, peeled cooking apple

grated rind of ½ lemon
1 egg
6fl oz/150ml medium dry cider or as
  needed (¾ cup)
butter for greasing

Rub the butter into the flour and salt. Shred the prepared apple, using the coarse holes on a grater. Add it to the flour and fat with the grated lemon rind. Stir in the egg, and enough cider to make a soft dough. Put it in a greased 8in x 4in x 2½in/200mm x 100mm x 65mm loaf tin, making sure you fill the corners. Level the top.

Bake at 375°F (190°C), Gas 5 for 45 minutes. Cool on a rack. Eat with cheese.

Note: Use 6oz/150g (1½ cups) each wholemeal and white self-raising flour if you cannot get 85 per cent flour.

BAKED OATMEAL BANNOCK *(Makes 1 round bannock — 8 wedges)*

Dripping is better than butter in these thick oatmeal scones, as well as being cheaper. Bacon dripping makes a more savoury bannock, but chicken fat makes a richer one — and one usually has more of it.

6oz/150g fine oatmeal (1 cup)
6oz/150g 85 per cent extraction
  flour (1½ cups)
1½ tsp baking powder (2 tsp)
½ tsp salt (¾ tsp)
pinch of ground allspice

½ tsp dried thyme or sage (¾ tsp)
4oz/100g chicken or bacon dripping,
  softened (½ cup)
cold water
bacon fat or margarine for greasing
melted butter for brushing (optional)

Shake all the dry ingredients together in a mixing bowl. Work in the fat until the mixture is crumbly. Mix in enough water to make a firm dough — about 2fl oz/50ml (¼ cup). On a meal-covered surface, shape or pat the dough into a flat round about ¾in/2cm thick. Put it on a lightly greased baking sheet, and brush the top with butter if you wish. Cut the round into 8 equal triangles, and separate them slightly.

Bake at 350°F (180°C), Gas 4 for 30–35 minutes. Eat warm for breakfast with butter and marmalade, or for supper with smoked Orkney cheese and tea or beer.

[90]

SAVOURY CORNMEAL BUNS *(makes 12–14 buns)*

The nineteenth-century radical, William Cobbett, spent nineteen years in America. When he returned to England, he tried hard to make working people grow maize, and published recipes using it — mostly, however, more solid than this modern one.

margarine for greasing
3 tbsp margarine (4 tbsp)
2 eggs
8 fl oz/200ml natural yoghurt
  (1 cup)
1 tsp clear honey (1 1/4 tsp)
6oz/150g wholewheat flour
  (1 1/2 cups)
4oz/100g plain white flour (1 cup)

2oz/50g cornmeal (polenta, maize
  meal) (1/2 cup)
1/2 tsp salt (3/4 tsp)
1 tsp baking powder (1 1/4 tsp)
1/2 tsp bicarbonate of soda (3/4 tsp
  baking soda)
2 crisp cooked bacon rashers, finely
  crumbled (2 strips)

Grease the insides of twelve 2½in/60mm bun tins about 1¼in/30mm deep. Melt the 3 tbsp (4 tbsp) margarine gently, without letting it get hot. Beat the eggs lightly into the yoghurt, add the honey, and stir into the melted fat. Shake together in a mixing bowl both flours, the cornmeal, salt, baking powder and soda. Add the finely crumbled bacon. Make a hollow in the middle and pour in the liquid, mixing in as quickly and lightly as you can.

Turn the mixture into the prepared bun tins, filling them only two-thirds full. Bake at 425°F (220°C), Gas 7 for 15–20 minutes. Cool on a rack. Eat with sausages, or use for a packed lunch with cheese.

[91]

BARLEY SCONES *(Makes 10 scones)*

A fatless version of these traditional scones used to be served with cider or ale to farmworkers on the threshing floor. In the dry, dusty atmosphere they must have produced a fine thirst! However, with a little fat, they make pleasantly nutty, sweetish brown scones, good for breakfast or at a mid-morning coffee (or cider) break.

6oz/150g barley flour (1½ cups)
2oz/50g plain white flour (½ cup)
pinch of salt
½ tsp bicarbonate of soda
 (½ tsp baking soda)
½ tsp cream of tartar (½ tsp)

1oz/25g butter (2 tbsp)
1oz/25g sieved muscovado sugar
 (2 tbsp)
4fl oz/100ml milk (½ cup)
egg yolk and water, beaten, for glazing
butter for greasing

Shake together the flours, salt and leavening in a bowl. Rub in the fat, then add the sugar. Mix to a soft dough with the milk. Pat out until ¾–1in/2–2.5cm thick. Cut out scones with a 2in/5cm cutter. Glaze the tops with egg yolk. Put on a greased baking sheet.

Bake at 425°F (220°C), Gas 7 for 10–12 minutes. Cool on the sheet. Serve split and buttered for breakfast, or with Apple Butter (page 110) and cider at midday.

BARNSTAPLE BUNS *(Makes 8–10 buns)*

Making conventional sweet buns with dripping helps to compensate for the cost of the dried fruit.

6oz/150g plain flour (1½ cups)
1 tsp baking powder (1¼ tsp)
pinch of salt
2oz/50g clarified dripping, not too
 hard (¼ cup)
3oz/75g caster sugar (¾ cup)

4oz/100g sultanas (½ cup)
grated rind of ½ small lemon
1 egg
2 tbsp milk or as needed (2½ tbsp)
butter or margarine for greasing

Sift the flour, baking powder and salt into a bowl. Rub in the fat until the mixture is crumbly. Mix in the other dry ingredients. Mix the egg with 1 tbsp (1¼ tbsp) milk, and bind the mixture to a spongy dough, adding the remaining milk if needed. Turn into well-greased, deep 2¾in/70mm bun tins, filling them three-quarters full.

Bake at 350°F (180°C), Gas 4 for about 25 minutes until risen and browned. Cool on a rack.

[92]

FRESH ORANGE BUNS *(Makes 16 buns)*

An unusual, pleasant way to include the full value of citrus fruit in everyday food.

1 medium orange
1 egg
6oz/150g natural golden
   granulated sugar (scant ¾ cup)
2 tbsp melted butter (2½ tbsp)
8fl oz/200ml milk (1 cup)

10oz/250g plain flour (2½ cups)
   (see method)
4 tsp baking powder (5 tsp)
¼ tsp salt (½ tsp)
butter for greasing

Cut the orange in pieces without peeling. Remove pips. Feed the orange into a food processor with the motor running. Blend until fully pulped. Turn into a small bowl.

Put the egg into the food processor, with the motor running, add the sugar, melted butter and milk. Stop the motor when fully blended.

Sift the flour onto paper, then remove 2 tsp (2½ tsp). Sift again into a bowl with the baking powder and salt. Make a well in the centre. Add a little of the egg mixture, and blend quickly. Add the remaining mixture and blend in using as few strokes as possible. Stir in the pulped orange.

Heat the oven to 400°F (200°C), Gas 6. Grease sixteen 3in x 1½in//75mm x 30mm deep bun tins. Fill two-thirds full with bun mixture. Bake for 30 minutes. Cool on a wire rack.

Serve while still warm, split and buttered, or reheat next day.

WHOLEMEAL GINGERBREAD *(Makes one 7¼–7½in/18–19cm gingerbread)*

Good with any spiced, stewed fruit such as plums, and equally good with Cheddar or soft white cheese, gingerbread is one of the most versatile of all baked goods.

butter for greasing
8oz/200g wholewheat flour
   (2 cups)
1½ tsp ground ginger (2 tsp)
1½ tsp baking powder (2 tsp)
½ tsp bicarbonate of soda
   (¾ tsp baking soda)
½ tsp salt (¾ tsp)
4oz/100g golden granulated sugar
   (½ cup)

3oz/75g clean dripping (good ⅓ cup)
3oz/75g molasses or natural pure cane
   syrup (¼ cup)
3oz/75g honey (¼ cup)
1 egg
½pt/250ml whole or skim milk
   (1¼ cups)

Grease and line a 7¼–7½in/180–190mm square Yorkshire pudding or baking tin.

[93]

Shake together in a bowl the flour, ground ginger, baking powder, bicarbonate of soda and salt. Put the sugar, fat, molasses and honey in a saucepan, and melt them without letting them get hot. Make a hollow in the dry ingredients and stir in the melted mixture. Beat thoroughly. Beat the egg into the milk, and add the liquid to the main mixture. Mix in, and beat for 2–3 minutes to blend thoroughly; the mixture will be quite liquid.

Pour the mixture into the prepared tin, and bake for 1 hour at 350°F (180°C), Gas 4, until firm and evenly risen. Cool in the tin; then turn out, wrap in clingfilm or foil, and store for at least 24 hours before cutting. Cut in fingers or squares as you prefer. Eat with cheese or with Apple Butter (page 110).

VICTORIAN COCONUT GINGERBREAD, 1845 (*Makes about 48 'breads'*)

Eliza Acton did not offer this as her cheapest gingerbread but did offer it as her very own. It contains no eggs and, as baked by Miss Acton, turns out to be small semi-hard biscuits (rock hard if overbaked). Gingerbread has always been made, more often than not, in the form of these small 'cakes' — but it is still called ginger*bread*.

10oz/250g plain flour (2½ cups)	*1lb/450g black treacle and golden*
6oz/150g rice flour (1½ cups)	*syrup, mixed (see note)*
grated rind of 1 lemon	*5oz/125g butter, chopped (½ cup +*
1½ tbsp ground ginger or to taste	*2 tbsp)*
(2 tbsp)	*5oz/125g desiccated coconut (1 cup +*
½ tsp bicarbonate of soda	*2 tbsp)*
(¾ tsp baking soda)	*fat for greasing*

Beat the first 5 ingredients together in a large bowl. Melt the treacle, syrup and butter in a saucepan. Pour them into the dry goods. Beat very thoroughly until smooth. Leave until quite cold. Mix in the coconut with a spoon or by hand. The dough must be stiffish. Put in small heaps on lightly greased baking sheets.

Bake at 300°F (150°C), Gas 2 for 30 minutes. The 'breads' will still be very soft. Loosen, and cool on the sheets, then store in an airtight tin.

Note: Use any proportions of treacle and syrup which are convenient; for instance if you have half a can of treacle to use up, make up the quantity with syrup, and include the last spoonfuls of a pot of honey if you want to.

USING BREAD

Fresh home-made bread, wholemeal especially, is so good that it seldom lasts long enough to go stale. However, you may sometimes have a loaf or a few slices of bread which are drier than they should be, or which you don't need because you are making fresh bread. You may find, too, that the last few buns of a batch, or rolls which you have served warmed at a dinner-party, get left in the bread bin, partly dried out. Don't throw them away. They can still be an asset because you can use them up in several ways.

Make, for instance, a bake-fried bread case, which looks like a golden coffer or bowl, and is a fine container for any hot filling. It can hold an everyday stew or fricassee, or make leftovers quite glamorous; you can eat the case itself instead of serving potatoes.

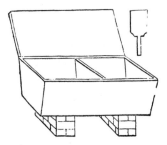

Stale round dinner rolls make attractive small cases for individual helpings. For less solid cases bake slices of buttered bread pressed into tartlet tins. Fried bread or toast slices are also the classic 'carriers' for small game birds, substantial savouries and rarebits, or, cut into fingers, serve as canapé bases.

If you have really dry bread, remember the merits of crumb pastry for making a case to hold a flan or quiche, or for a cheesecake base. You can make a crumb 'mix' whenever you happen to have the bread, and freeze it until you need it. You can add nutrients and interest to it with crushed nuts, cheese, herbs or jam just before baking.

Bread can also be used up, sliced or crumbled, in many other ways. A few spoonfuls of breadcrumbs always lighten suet crust pastry. Bread or crumbs also make good savoury dishes such as Rabbit Layers (page 61), or sweet ones such as the Guard's Pudding (page 98).

BREADCRUMB PASTRY 'MIX'

2oz/50g unsalted butter (¹/₄ cup)
4oz/100g stale white or wholemeal bread, finely crumbled (2 cups)

Melt the fat in a frying pan. Turn the crumbs in the fat until evenly coated all over but not coloured. Cool on soft kitchen paper, then store in a dry, closed jar in the refrigerator.

Before use, bring to room temperature. Add any flavourings your recipe requires, and any extra fat needed to make the crumbs cohere when pressed. They should still be crumbly rather than pasty.

BREADCRUMB PASTRY FLAN CASE *(Makes one 8¹/₂–9in/ 210–225mm case)*

8oz/200g stale breadcrumbs, white or wholemeal (4 cups)
2 tbsp crushed nuts, wheatgerm or similar solid nutrient (2¹/₂ tbsp)
1–2oz/25–50g sugar, or to taste, for sweet pastry (2–4 tbsp)

4oz/100g butter or other fat suited to filling (¹/₂ cup)
flavouring(s), eg spices, to taste
fat for greasing (as above)

Mix the crumbs evenly with any solid 'extras' and sugar if used. Warm the fat gently in a saucepan, and remove from the heat as soon as it has melted. Cool for 2–3 minutes; then mix with the crumbs, adding any other flavourings. Press the mixture evenly and firmly over the sides and base of a greased flan case or plain (not fluted) ring on a baking sheet. Cover the sides first, fairly thickly; the bottom can be patched with biscuit, crispbread or other crumbs if too thin.

Trim the top edges of the case with a sharp knife, slicing off any ragged bits. Brush off loose crumbs. Chill for 10–20 minutes, then bake blind for 15–20 minutes at 370°F (190°C), Gas 5 until slightly crisp with a browned rim. Cool before use.

Note: For a cheesecake base, press pastry over the base only of your chosen container. Unlike most biscuit-crumb 'carriers', it should be baked before use.

Variation:
You can add up to 2oz/50g (½ cup) grated hard cheese to the breadcrumbs but use only 3oz/75g (⅓ cup) fat.

PLOUGHMAN'S OMELETTE

For each omelette, cut a large, square, crustless slice of stale bread into ¼in/5mm dice. Moisten them with Garlic Oil (page 148) or butter, then fry or bake until crisp and golden.

Make the omelette in the usual way, adding half the fried dice to the batter before frying. When the omelette is cooked, sprinkle the remaining dice over it together with chopped fresh herbs such as chives, or with chopped fried onion. Fold and serve sprinkled with grated cheese and chives.

WALNUT AND SULTANA PUDDING *(Serves 4–6)*

4 large slices bread and butter
butter for greasing
2oz/50g chopped walnuts (½ cup)
2oz/50g sultanas (½ cup golden
* raisins)*

2 eggs
2½oz/65g sugar (¼ cup + 1 tbsp)
¾pt/375ml hot milk (2 cups)
redcurrant jelly

Cut the bread and butter slices in half and arrange them in a lightly greased 1½pt/850ml (2pt) deep pie dish or oven-to-table baking dish. Sprinkle each layer with a few nuts and sultanas, using half the total quantity. Beat together the eggs and sugar, and add the hot milk. Pour over the dish, and sprinkle the remaining nuts and sultanas on top.

Bake at 350°F (180°C), Gas 4 for 45 minutes. Serve hot, with a dollop of redcurrant jelly on each helping.

BROWN BETTY *(Serves 4–6)*

You will find versions of this traditional apple dessert throughout the world. This one was taken to America by the Pilgrim Fathers, and has now come back to us.

6 Granny Smith apples
6oz/150g golden granulated
* sugar (¾ cup)*
½ tsp ground cinnamon (¾ tsp)
¼ tsp each ground cloves and
* grated nutmeg (¼ tsp each)*
¼ tsp salt (½ tsp)

grated rind of ½ lemon
1 tbsp butter for greasing (1¼ tbsp)
2oz/50g butter, melted
6oz/150g fresh white breadcrumbs
* (3 cups)*
2 tbsp lemon juice (2½ tbsp)

Peel and core the apples and slice them thinly. Mix together the golden granulated sugar, spices, salt and lemon rind. Grease a shallow 8½in/210mm baking dish with melted butter. Mix the 2oz/50g (¼ cup) butter with the breadcrumbs, coating them well.

[97]

Sprinkle one-third of the breadcrumb mixture over the base of the dish. Spread half the sliced apples over the crumbs, and sprinkle with 1 tablespoon lemon juice. Cover with half the spiced sugar, and another third of the crumbs. Repeat the apple layer. Sprinkle over it the second tablespoon of lemon juice then trickle into the dish ⅛pt/ 65ml (good ¼ cup) warm water. Cover the apples with the remaining sugar and crumbs. Lay a sheet of foil loosely on top.

Bake at 350°F (180°C), Gas 4 for 30 minutes. Uncover, and bake for 15 minutes until the top is crusty and the sauce well reduced. Raise the heat to 425°F (220°C), Gas 7 and bake for another 6–7 minutes to brown the top. Serve hot with chilled whipped cream.

GUARD'S PUDDING *(Serves 4–6)*

6oz/150g fine wholemeal
breadcrumbs (3 cups)
pinch of salt
4oz/100g butter or margarine,
well softened (½ cup)
4oz/100g muscovado sugar
(½ cup)

3 tbsp smooth or sieved strawberry
jam (scant 4 tbsp)
1 tsp bicarbonate of soda
(1¼ tsp baking soda)
1 egg
strawberry purée or jam as sauce
(see method)

Grease a 1½pt/850ml (2pt) pudding basin. Mix together all the ingredients except the bicarbonate and egg. Whisk the bicarbonate into the egg, and stir into the pudding. Turn into the basin, cover

securely with greased foil, and steam in a pan of boiling water for 3 hours. The water should come half-way up the basin's sides and be topped up with extra boiling water if needed.

Let the pudding stand in the basin, off the heat, for 5 minutes, when done. Then unmould it onto a warmed serving dish, and serve with a hot strawberry sauce.

For the sauce you can, if you wish, purée fresh, frozen or canned strawberries with a little white wine or natural apple juice, adding a spoonful of caster sugar (optional); just warm the mixture gently in a saucepan. Alternatively sieve and warm with a little water almost a full 1lb/454g pot of strawberry jam, (perhaps the rest of a pot opened to make the pudding). A real egg custard would be quite a good alternative if you have no fruit or jam.

POOR KNIGHTS OF WINDSOR *(Serves 4)*

A dish with a remarkable history! Edward III founded a society or corporation of poor, honourable old soldiers called 'poor knights' in 1348, and the dish seems to be associated with them, or perhaps with Crusaders generally because every country in Europe and a good many farther off have their own traditional versions. This is an old English one from Berkshire.

4 large slices stale white bread,   *unsalted butter for frying*
    ¹/₂in/1cm thick   *red jam or jelly, or 4 tsp caster sugar*
4 tbsp milk sweetened to taste   *and 1 tsp ground cinnamon*
    (5 tbsp)   *(5 tsp/1¹/₂ tsp)*
1 egg and 1 yolk beaten together

Cut the crusts off the bread. Moisten the slices with the sweetened milk without making them soggy. Dip in beaten egg, coating both sides well. Fry gently in butter, turning once, until golden on both sides. Serve hot with a spoonful of jam or jelly on each slice, or sprinkled with sugar and cinnamon.

Other versions use port or sweet wine instead of milk, a thin batter — sometimes with blanched flaked almonds in it, or honey instead of sugar. I have read that in India the milk is flavoured with almonds and the 'toasts' are served with wedges of lime.

6
SPREADS FOR YOUR BREAD

—◆◆—

'A good spread' doesn't only mean a super schoolboy tea although tasty 'spreadables' often find a place in one. Well-flavoured foods made into a paste are more prized however for packed and snack meals, now part of many, perhaps most, people's regular eating pattern. Field and office workers, mothers lunching with toddlers, teenagers home from school before working parents return, are just some of them. Supermarkets sell a mass of packeted spreads, but home-made ones are more trustworthy and cheaper.

A good spread starts with good basic products, not ill-assorted scraps. You can use pre-cooked food or leftovers, but make sure that the spread still has food value as well as flavour. Don't, for instance, pound yesterday's stew to a paste for tomorrow's sandwiches — most of its goodness went into the gravy.

Your spreads and fillings will almost certainly be 'carried' by bread or pastry in some form, so try to use protein or vegetable ingredients rather than starchy ones. Pulses are an exception because they contain good secondary proteins, and are ideal for 'binding' loose bits of meat or vegetable without using quantities of butter or mayonnaise. Home-made mayonnaise can be delicious but remember its fatty egg content and don't overdo other fats when you use it. If you make a spread containing mayonnaise for sandwiches, for instance, don't butter the bread; a scraping of low-fat curd cheese will do just as well. You'll feel slenderer and a few pennies richer.

Both for health reasons and to cut cost, consider fats other than butter for sandwich spreads. Margarine is not the only alternative. Victorian cooks certainly made do without it: one got bread-and-jam or dripping toast on butterless days, and a currant dripping cake instead of bread-and-butter on Sundays. I was regretful to find recently that my own, now grown-up, children had completely forgotten dripping toast, and that other young adults looked at me blankly when I mentioned dripping cakes (page 174). Yet these still make a satisfying 'cut-and-come-again' tea-time filler. The dripping from your roast meat or poultry has excellent flavour value too as a topping for vegetables, for frying foods like Potato Cakes (page 138) or for making savoury omelettes and so on.

Beef dripping is not the only kind you can use. Lamb or venison dripping tends to taste tallowy, but pork, sausage and poultry (chicken or turkey) drippings are delicious. The French, being thrifty, also make good use of the quantities of rich fat from a roast duck or goose for their famous 'confits'. Faggots (page 30) are especially good when fried in sausage or bacon fat and so are chicken livers, mushrooms or bubble-and-squeak. These fats can often replace butter; in particular, use the stronger-flavoured fats for making poultry or game pâtés or potted spreads (but not for sealing them unless you clarify the fat first).

Clarifying dripping is simple, and so is rendering down your own pork fat for lard, and beef fat for suet. The method is the same for them all.

To render/clarify fats

Use the fat from roast beef, pork, or poultry, bacon, ham or sausage for dripping. Use hard uncooked beef fat for suet. Hard pork kidney fat or excess fat pared off pork before cooking makes lard.

Chop the fat into small pieces without bothering to remove tag-ends of skin or bits of gristle. Pour 1/4in/5mm water into a baking tin, add the fat in a thin layer, and bake gently until any scraps of skin and gristle are shrunken and crisp with all the spare fat melted out of them. Turn the whole contents of the tin into a sieve placed over a bowl. Press any scraps in the sieve with the back of a spoon to squeeze out the last few drops of fat, then discard if gristly. (Use plain crisp skin as for Chicken Crisps, page 45.)

Cool the fat until solid, then loosen the block of fat from the bowl with a knife. Pour off any water underneath and, in the case of dripping, scrape the bottom of the block free of any solid gravy sticking to it. According to the kind of fat you used to start with, you will have rendered pure lard, suet or clarified dripping.

When you get dripping from a roast, you generally get a lot of it. Its shelf-life is fairly short, and a spoonful or two on vegetables or used for frying may not make any real inroads into your supply. Rather than waste it, try using it to make the dripping cakes I've mentioned, and buns and pastry — in other words, 'carriers' for your spreads. They are often more satisfying and warming in packed meals than lighter, ordinary breads.

Meat, fish, cheese and vegetable pastes are the commonest savoury spreads, although looser mixtures of cooked egg, shredded hard cheese or chopped vegetables held together by thick sauce are often used too. Soft cheeses, especially with vegetables, fruit or herbs added, make another main group. Then there are the savoury butters, extravagant but certainly spreadable, pickles and chutneys, jams, marmalade and the fruit pastes called 'butters' and 'cheeses'. Among these you should find a classic combination or a guide to using successfully any ingredients you have available. The recipes given below are samples from each of the main types of 'spreadables'. They're not necessarily economical products; some are frankly luxuries. but a little of any spread goes a long way, and the better it is, the further its rich, concentrated flavour goes.

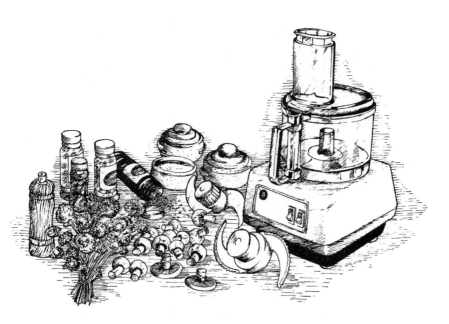

PÂTÉS AND POTTED FOODS

Spare and leftover foods, especially meats, have for centuries been made into spiced pastes sealed under a layer of fat to preserve them. French cooks used lard or goose fat, and called their products pâtés — that is, food 'pounded to paste'. The English, alone in Europe, used butter — from the time of their eighteenth-century dairying boom onward. They put their meat and fish pastes into small, deep crocks or pots, sealed them under a rich golden layer of clarified butter, and called them 'potted beef', 'potted shrimps' and so on.

This use of butter to make meat, fish and vegetable preserves is extravagant today when freezers and cans do it more securely. As a way of making unappealing offals or leftovers tasty, it is usually a failure. As a way of making the most of butter and of making a luxurious, easily served product which is all your own work, potting is unrivalled. There are no real recipes for this old craft, only guidelines; in no other branch of cookery does your personal taste and touch matter so much. It lets you make the very most of your cookery flair. Really for this reason, I have sneaked in here, on the excuse that they make superb spreads, a few butter-sealed potted foods as well as more plebeian but thrifty fat-sealed pâtés.

One word of warning. These so-called preserves are not such

[103]

reliable keepers as their history may make you believe. Our homes are warmer than in the past, and many of our food animals have been artificially fed or inoculated, and their flesh is soft and moist. Cool any meat rapidly if to be used cold, and refrigerate any pâté from the time you make it until you use it.

POTTING-JAR

POTTED BEEF

The original recipe used raw shin of beef, well wrapped and baked in the cooling bread oven for several hours. Today, you could cook it in a slow cooker or at the special slow setting on some ovens (eg Flavel). If you have a solid fuel stove, bake it overnight in the old way.

1lb/450g cooked shin of beef
*   without gristle, cubed*
4oz/100g butter (1/2 cup)
3–4 tsp anchovy sauce or a little
*   anchovy essence (5 tsp)*
1/2–1 tsp each white pepper and
*   ground mace (3/4–1 1/4 tsp)*

good pinch of grated nutmeg
salt, pepper and cayenne to taste
3–4 small lumps or 1–2 tsp sugar,
*   to taste (1 1/4–2 1/2 tsp)*
hard pork fat, melted (see method)

Render the hard pork fat for sealing by chopping it into small pieces and putting these in a baking tin in a low oven until you have small crisp 'scratchings' and liquid fat. Drain the fat well and refrigerate for use when required.

Mince and pound the beef, or chop it and reduce it to paste in a food processor, with a little of the butter. Put the remaining butter and most of each of the flavourings, including the sugar, into a saucepan, and heat gently until the butter and sugar melt. Work in the meat paste, then heat through well, stirring continuously. Taste and add extra flavouring as needed.

Press into small pots, tapping once or twice on the table while filling, to pack the paste down solidly. Leave a good 1/2in/1cm headspace. Wipe the rims of the pots, then seal with a thin layer of melted fat. Leave until cold and firm, then re-seal to cover any hair cracks. Store, covered, in the refrigerator.

Spread thickly in sandwiches, and cover with thinly sliced cucumber or stoned, sliced black olives.

[104]

ENGLISH POTTED PORK OR BACON

1lb/450g cold boiled pork or bacon
3oz/75g butter (use unsalted
  butter with bacon) (¹/₃ cup)
salt to taste

good pinch each of grated onion
  and dried sage with pork, or of
  ground mace with bacon
hard back pork fat, melted

Mince the meat and pound with butter and seasonings, or reduce to paste in a food processor. Taste and add extra seasonings if needed.

Press into pots, tapping on the table-top once or twice to pack the paste down solidly. Leave at least ½in/1cm headspace. Cover with a thin layer of melted fat. When firm, seal with a second layer. Cool, then cover and refrigerate until needed. Leave to stand at room temperature for 20 minutes before use.

LIVER PÂTÉ

The classic, and perhaps still the best, way to use liver is in a pâté.

1lb/450g pigs' liver
4oz/100g lean bacon, without rind
1 small onion
2oz/50g bacon fat (¹/₄ cup)
1oz/25g margarine (2 tbsp)
2 hard-boiled egg yolks, crumbled

salt and ground black pepper
pinch of chopped fresh sage or
  powdered dried sage
3 bay leaves (optional)
clarified butter or melted hard pork
  fat as needed

Chop the liver, bacon and onion into small pieces. Sauté gently in the mixed fats for 4 minutes only. (Or, if you prefer, cook the liver and bacon, and then chop.) Mince and pound the liver, bacon, onion and egg yolks, or reduce to paste in a food processor. Moisten with a little fat from the pan to taste; season well. Mix in the sage.

Grease a shallow baking dish with a little more frying fat, and turn in the mixture. Level and smooth the top. Arrange the bay leaves, if used, in a trefoil pattern in the centre. Cover tightly with greased foil, and stand the dish in a pan containing a little hot water. Bake at 350°F (180°C), Gas 4 for 45 minutes. Cool. When cold, cover with melted clarified butter or pork fat. When this is firm, re-seal with a little more fat. Allow this to firm up, then cover and refrigerate.

Before using, take off the hard fat covering; it should lift off quite easily. The pâté can then be served from the dish as a first course with its trefoil of bay leaves as decoration, or it can be used for sandwiches.

For a party pâté, you could add 2 tsp (1 tbsp) brandy and 3–4 tsp (2 tbsp) single (light) cream with the egg yolks.

[105]

POTTED SMOKED HADDOCK

1lb/450g cooked smoked haddock,   *good pinch each of mixed spice, white*
   skinned and boned   *pepper and grated nutmeg*
2–3oz/50–75g butter (¹/₄–¹/₃ cup)   *melted clarified butter*

Pound the fish, butter and flavourings, or reduce to paste in a food
processor. Taste and add extra flavourings if you wish. Pot and
cover with clarified butter, as for Potted Beef (page 104).

PESTLE AND MORTAR.

POTTED MUSHROOMS

1lb/450g button mushrooms   *¹/₄ tsp ground allspice (¹/₂ cup)*
2oz/50g unsalted butter (¹/₄ cup)   *a few drops of Worcester sauce*
salt and freshly ground black   *3 anchovy fillets*
   pepper   *clarified butter as needed*

Chop the mushrooms and stems finely. Put them in a dry saucepan,
cover, and simmer gently for about 10 minutes until the juice is running freely. Raise the heat, uncover, and continue cooking until the
liquid has evaporated. Stir in the butter, seasoning, spice and sauce.
Continue cooking until the mushrooms have absorbed the fat.

Meanwhile, chop or mince the anchovy fillets finely. Stir into the
mushrooms and cook for 2–3 minutes longer. Press the mixture into
a small pot and cover with clarified butter. Cool, cover and store.
Use within one month.

Note: This is a good way to use a sudden big crop of Sofa Mushrooms (page 137).

OTHER SPREADS FOR SANDWICHES AND CANAPÉS

——◆◇◆——

Good spreads for use as sandwich fillings can be made of almost any nourishing spare food you have to hand, provided you prepare it wisely. But any filling must meet these conditions:

1 Avoid making flaky fillings. A sandwich filled with a thick layer of coarsely grated cheese looks lavish, but the same quantity of cheese in a thin, solid slice is much less messy and more satisfying to munch. Lettuce shreds are difficult to bite off cleanly, and tend to pull out of a sandwich in ribbons.

2 For 'finger food', a filling should be fairly firm and dry. A drooping sandwich tends to shed its contents. (Damp vol-au-vents which give way underneath do so too.) For this reason, avoid making fillings with foods or sauces which may give off liquid when left to 'stand'.

3 If you want to heat the filling, say for toasted sandwiches, it must not curdle, toughen, or melt enough to run out in the process. Fillings bound with yoghurt, fat, and some cheeses can be risky. Avoid fillings made of loose 'bits' bound with a sauce which will melt, especially for finger food.

When you make your own fillings, try to contrast flavour and texture. Spread sandwiches with chutney instead of fat, for instance, if you use a cheese filling. Bind white chicken meat, which is dryish, with a creamy sauce or soft cheese; mix hard-boiled egg with capers or bind it with a dressing containing grated horseradish.

Fruit spreads

In summer you can make without stint the best fruit spreads and fillings of all simply by puréeing fruit and perhaps simmering it down with a little honey until almost pasty. But in the sunless days when we need all the vitamins and fresh flavours we can get, there may be hardly any fruit, and that little is expensive. Storing summer fruit therefore makes sense, whether you freeze, dry, bottle or just stack it in a yard or outhouse.

But other foods also make claims on available freezer space — and drying fruit such as apple rings is laborious and no longer cheap, as it was when cooks used a cooling wood-burning oven after baking.

[107]

Bottling can also be high on fuel and equipment costs, and the bottles take up valuable storage space in a small kitchen. Stacking either fruit or vegetables is only 'on' if you have a suitable, fairly large space, indoors or outdoors. For a small household, then, making condensed preserves such as whole fruit jams and chutneys may be the only practical way to preserve them. They will lack vitamin C and may be very sweet, but they will have fibre and natural flavour.

Here are a few recipes for jams and similar fruit preserves, followed by some vegetable spreads and 'dips'. Recipes for fruit pickles and chutneys which are not 'spreadables' are in Chapter 10.

RHUBARB.

SPICED RHUBARB JAM *(makes about 6lb/2.5kg)*
A glut of summer garden rhubarb is not unusual. Turn the thick juicy stalks into this flavoursome preserve for use in winter flans and tarts. It sets less firmly than most jams.

3¹/₂lb/1.5kg rhubarb
3 tbsp lemon juice (4 tbsp)
3¹/₂lb/1.5kg sugar (7 cups)
¹/₂oz/15g piece dried ginger root,
  soaked overnight

2–3 whole cloves
1in/2.5cm piece of cinnamon stick

String the rhubarb if coarse and cut into 1in/2.5cm pieces. Sprinkle with the lemon juice. Layer the fruit and sugar in a preserving pan, cover and leave for several hours or overnight. Next morning bruise the ginger root and tie it in a thin cloth, together with the cloves and cinnamon stick. Add to the fruit.

Bring to the boil over medium heat and boil fast until you have about 3¹/₄ pt/1.8 litres jam (before making the jam, pour 3¹/₄ pt/1.8 litres water into the empty pan and mark the level). Remove from the heat and discard spices. Spoon the jam into warmed jars and cover loosely with waxed paper discs. Seal when cold; then label with name and date, and store in a cool place.

[108]

BLACKBERRY AND APPLE JAM *(makes about 6lb/2.5kg)*
A late summer jam. Use cultivated blackberries unless the year's
hedgerow fruit is unusually large and juicy.

14oz/375g cooking apples, peeled, *12fl oz/300ml water (1½ cups)*
  cored and sliced *2lb/900g blackberries*
1 strip lemon peel *3½lb/1.5kg sugar (7 cups)*

Cook the apples with the lemon peel in 6fl oz/150ml of the water
until very soft and pulpy. Separately, cook the blackberries in the
remaining water until tender. Mix the fruits in a preserving pan; discard the peel and add the sugar.

Place over low heat, and stir until the sugar dissolves. Raise the
heat, and boil quickly without stirring until a little jam sets on a cold
plate. Remove from the heat. Spoon the jam into warmed jars, cover
with circles of waxed paper. Seal when cold, label with name and
date, and store in a cool place.

SEVILLE ORANGE MARMALADE *(Makes 9–10lb/4–4.5kg)*

The tang of good home-made marmalade is unmatched by any jam. This recipe makes the most of bitter Seville oranges, turning them into a delicious preserve with dozens of uses, in savoury dishes as well as sweet ones. Traditionally British, it is a product that the Scots, in particular, rightly take pride in.

3lb/1.3kg Seville oranges
6pt/3 litres water (7¹/₂pt)

juice of 2 lemons
6lb/2.5kg preserving sugar (12 cups)

Take off the whole orange peel, cutting it into ¼in/5mm-wide strips. Put the peel in a pan with half the water and the strained lemon juice. Bring to the boil, and simmer, covered, for 2 hours until the peel is tender.

Cut up the orange flesh, and put in a second pan with the remaining water. Bring to the boil, cover and simmer for 1½ hours. Strain the liquid from the pulped flesh over the soft peel.

Bring the mixture to the boil and simmer for 10 minutes. Stir in the sugar. Raise the heat and boil rapidly without stirring until the temperature reaches setting point (220°F/104°C). Skim well, and let the marmalade stand, off the heat, for about 30 minutes, stirring occasionally.

Pour into heated, dry jars, and cover with waxed paper discs, treated side down. When cold, cover with cellophane or greaseproof paper. Store in a cool place. Will keep for a year.

APPLE BUTTER

This is a good way to use up windfalls and withered apples. It is not worth making with less than 4lb/1.8kg, but you can use any convenient larger quantity.

hot water or cider to cover base of
*   pan (see method)*
¹/₄–¹/₂lb/100–200g granulated
*   sugar (¹/₂–1 cup) per 1pt/500ml*
*   pulp (2¹/₂ cups)*

chosen quantity of apples
¹/₄ tsp ground cinnamon (¹/₂ tsp) per
*   1pt/500ml pulp (2¹/₂ cups)*
good pinch of ground cloves per
*   1pt/500ml pulp (2¹/₂ cups)*

Cut out bruised and bad portions of apples, but do not core or peel them. Chop them roughly. Place in a large iron or earthenware ovenproof crock with enough hot water or cider to give 3in/7.5cm depth. Cover the crock with aluminium foil, then with a lid or plate. Place it in the oven at a very low heat, 225°F (110°C), Gas ¼, and leave for 5 hours or overnight.

Sieve the soft apples and measure the pulp. (This easily made pulp also makes an excellent purée for apple sauce or for a flan filling.) Add the sugar to the pulp and stir well. Place over moderate heat, bring to the boil, and simmer for ¾–1 hour until the 'butter' is thick and dark, stirring in the spices after about 30 minutes.

When ready, remove the apple pulp from the heat, and spoon into hot jars. (Use jars without shoulders if possible.) Leave until cold. Cover with waxed circles of paper, then with airtight lids. Label with name and date.

This butter should ideally be kept for several months before use, and can be kept for two years. Like a fruit 'cheese', it is stiffer than jam, and becomes stiffer and spicier with age.

SPICED PLUM 'CHEESE'

A fruit 'butter' or 'cheese' has more concentrated fresh fruit in it than jam, and is more satisfying.

Cut up the plums roughly. Bake them with very little water in a sealed pot overnight, at the lowest possible temperature, to make a purée. Sieve and cool it, then make your 'cheese'.

1pt/500ml unsweetened plum purée (2½ cups) *10–12oz/250–300g muscovado sugar, or to taste (1¼–1½ cups)*	*¼ tsp ground cloves (½ tsp)* *½ tsp ground cinnamon (¾ tsp)* *1 tsp lemon juice, optional (1¼ tsp)* *glycerine for smearing jars*

Heat jars without shoulders and with screw-on or spring-clip lids. Put the purée, sugar and spices into a heavy saucepan. Bring gently to the boil, stirring. Then cook gently, stirring at intervals, for about 50 minutes or until the purée is as thick as soft cheese and makes a heavy plopping sound. Taste then add the lemon juice and any extra spices you wish. Continue cooking until the spoon leaves a clean line if drawn across the bottom of the pan.

Stand the hot jars on thick newspaper. Smear their insides with glycerine, and fill them as soon as you take the pan off the stove; the purée stiffens quickly. Cover the filled jars loosely with circles of waxed paper or stout paper dipped in brandy. When cold, fit screw-on or lug-top lids and label.

You can use the preserve like jam after 2–3 weeks, or keep it for several months; it should then be solid enough to turn out and cut in slices like pâté or cheese.

[111]

LEMON CURD *(Makes about 12oz/300g [1½ cups])*

This is an unusually economical recipe for lemon curd, but hard to beat.

3oz/75g margarine (⅓ cup)
9oz/225g caster sugar (1 cup +
2 tbsp)

grated rind and juice of 3 lemons
3 large (size 2) eggs, beaten

Put the margarine, sugar, lemon rind and juice in the top part of a double boiler over medium heat. Stir until the sugar dissolves, then boil without stirring for 3–5 minutes. Cool, then strain to remove the rind. Stir in the beaten eggs.

Again place over medium heat in the double boiler, and stir until the mixture thickens; do not let it boil. Pour the curd into warmed, sterilised jars. Cover with waxed paper, treated side down; when cool, put on a cellophane cover. Refrigerate, or store in a cool place, and use within 3 weeks.

MOCK MARRON

This old French recipe for a sweet bean conserve promised that it would taste just like sweetened chestnut purée. I make no such bold claim, but it is certainly a delicious and cheap sweet preserve.

two 15oz/425g cans butter or
cannellini beans, drained
one 7½/213g can butter or
cannellini beans, drained

1lb/500g white sugar (2 cups)
¼ pt/125ml water (½ cup + 2 tbsp)
1 vanilla pod, split lengthways

Purée the drained beans in a food processor or blender until smooth. Put the sugar, water and vanilla pod in a heavy saucepan or preserving pan. Heat slowly, stirring, until the sugar dissolves. Add the beans. Bring back to simmering point and simmer gently, uncovered, for 45 minutes. Stir from time to time towards the end, when the purée thickens and darkens slightly. When ready, the conserve will just have begun to dry at the sides of the pan.

Pour the conserve into warmed clean jars, and cover the surface with waxed paper discs. Cool, seal like jam, label with name and date. Store for not more than 1 week in the refrigerator, or freeze.

Vegetable Spreads and Dips
The spreads which follow will each make 4–6 average-sized sandwiches or rolls, depending on how thickly you fill them. One or two dips are included because toast or vegetable 'dunkers' serve the same purpose as bread or toast used as sandwiches — they are 'carriers' for the savoury food.

TOMATO AND CHEESE SPREAD

1 small onion
4 medium tomatoes
1oz/25g butter (2 tbsp)
1 large or 2 small eggs
2oz/50g mild Cheddar cheese,
  shredded

3–4oz/75–100g fresh white
  breadcrumbs (1½–2 cups)
salt and pepper

Skin the onion and grate or chop it finely. Chop the tomatoes roughly. Melt the butter in a pan, add the onion and tomatoes, and simmer for 20 minutes. Remove from heat. Beat the egg or eggs until liquid and add gradually to the simmered mixture, stirring continuously to prevent curdling. If the mixture does not thicken, return the pan to very gentle heat for a moment or two, and stir until it does.
  Sieve into a bowl while still hot, stir in the cheese and enough breadcrumbs to make a thick paste. Season to taste. Cool thoroughly, then pot like Potted Beef (page 104). Keep in the refrigerator until required.

POTATO AND PEPPER SPREAD *(Makes 12fl oz/300ml [1½ cups])*
Even leftover cold potato tastes good this way!

1 green pepper, 4oz/100g
½ medium onion, about 2oz/50g
1 clove garlic (optional)
1 large boiled potato, 8oz/200g

½ tsp salt (¾ tsp)
1 tbsp lemon juice (1¼ tbsp)
3 tbsp mayonnaise (4 tbsp)

Seed and chop the pepper. Chop the onion and squeeze the garlic clove (if used) over it. Cube the potato. With the motor running, put all the ingredients except the potato in an electric blender. Process until smooth, then add the potato and blend for a second or two. Take care not to overblend and make the potato 'gluey'. Turn into a carton and chill until needed.

SALAD SANDWICH SPREAD

2 large stalks celery, chopped
2 carrots, about 3oz/75g each,
  sliced
3 large radishes, sliced
1/2 green pepper, cored, seeded
  and chopped

2 tbsp mayonnaise or as needed
  (2 1/2 tbsp)
salt and pepper

Mince all the vegetables together or, better, put them in order into a food processor with the motor running, and grind finely. Bind with mayonnaise and season to taste.

AUBERGINE (EGGPLANT) SPREAD OR DIP *(Makes 14fl oz/ 350ml [1 3/4 cups])*

one 12oz/300g aubergine
  (eggplant)
2oz/50g ground almonds (1/2 cup)

8oz/200g natural cottage cheese
  (1 cup)
2 tbsp lemon juice (2 1/2 tbsp)

Cut the aubergine in half lengthways. Place both halves, cut side down, under the grill. Grill, turning once or twice, until the aubergine flesh is soft. Cool, then strip off the skin. Cut in chunks.

With the motor running, put all the ingredients in order into a food processor or blender and process until smooth. Turn into a container and chill until needed.

Note: This is a delicately flavoured soft spread or dip. It would make a beautiful coating for cold chicken. Serve a light dry white wine with it.

HAM AND SPRING ONION DIP

9oz/225g full fat soft ('cream')
  cheese (1 cup + 2 tbsp)
1 1/2 tbsp finely chopped spring
  onion green (2 tbsp)

4–6 tsp milk (5–7 tsp)
pinch of salt
2–3oz/50–75g pork luncheon meat,
  finely shredded

Cream the cheese in a bowl with the back of a spoon. Mix in all the other ingredients. Add extra milk if you want a more liquid 'dip'.

As 'dunkers', use 3in/7.5cm lengths of scraped celery, scraped young carrots and 'sticks' of quartered cucumber.

7

VEGETABLES IN PLENTY

—◆◇◆—

Vegetables are cheap, filling, good to taste and good for you; so making the most of them means making sure that you have plenty whenever you want them, at their peak of flavour and food value.

Countless magazine articles and books (and a growing number of vocal vegetarians) have in recent years put vegetable cookery on the map, and so most of us have some idea of how we should treat vegetables to enjoy them at their best. But the 'rules' are worth repeating because it's all too easy — since vegetables seldom demand attention while cooking — just to let them go on simmering in a pan on the stove while we do something else, as generations of cooks have done before us.

Handling vegetables is one area of cookery — the only one — in which the traditional methods and dishes of the past teach us nothing and give us no help at all. In fact ignore them, and focus instead of these modern ideas.

Eat vegetables as soon as you can after you get them. If you grow them, take them straight from the garden to the pot, or to the table. If you buy them, do so if possible on the day you will eat them; they start losing vitamins as soon as they are gathered.

Ideally, gather or buy young vegetables with tender skins. The vitamins of many vegetables lie just under the outer surface, so peel them only if their skins are hard or tough.

[115]

Serve salads whenever you can. Young vegetables, especially, taste their best and have most food value when raw or just blanched. Only wash vegetables just before you use them. Never let them soak in water, especially if cut up. Water leaches out their vitamins. Serve vegetables whole whenever you can. Make labour-saving a virtue. If you must process them, do no more than you need. Halve rather than cube, cube rather than dice, them. Every cut surface loses vitamins.

Cut surfaces *go on* shedding vitamins, so only cut the vegetables just before you cook or serve them. If you cook them, choose the methods which take least time, or which seal the surfaces. Boil quickly and briefly, or sauté or stir-fry. All vegetables are best served still crisp — what traditionalists call half-cooked.

Cook vegetables at the last moment before the meal. Lying about in a vegetable dish does nothing for their nutrient value or their texture and flavour.

These are purists' rules. Almost certainly, you won't be able to follow them rigidly: only a few devoted gardeners can live on just-ripe vegetables brought from garden to table within an hour. For most of us, vegetables come from shop or supermarket, have been grown for looks, harvested for keeping, and processed for packaging, if only by cutting off their leafy tops or roots. We have to do our best with them by cooking them shrewdly. Even those of us who have gardens cannot often achieve the ideal. Vegetable crops have an annoying habit of dawdling unripe, then making a growth spurt all together so that one week there's almost nothing to harvest, and the next there's a glut. Inevitably, some vegetables are left in the ground or on the vine until past their prime.

Nonetheless, give the vegetables you get the best treatment you can. Just blanch them for salads or 'short-cook' firm-fresh ones, for instance as in the recipes beginning on page 128. Try stir-frying if you haven't already done so; it is a colourful process — fun for the cook as well as the consumers — and the very brief cooking compensates for the fact that you have to cut the vegetables into small bits or shred them. If you don't already know it, try what the Japanese call nabé or one-pot cookery, which is like stir-frying, only often uses stock instead of fat.

Raspberry Pot Pie, page 160 *(Butter Information Council)*

[116]

As for those older and glut vegetables, home-grown or from the supermarket, remember that you will make much better use of vegetables if you have them available whenever you want them. Sensible storage is one answer to that problem. A garden or allotment owner can make an outdoor storage stack for root vegetables. The owner of a terraced house probably can't, but may have cellar space he can set aside, or a large freezer. A flat-dweller may have none of these things, so making mild or sweet pickles and chutneys may be his best bet (and incidentally is a good way of relieving pressure on freezer space too). There's even a case for using commercially canned, frozen or dried vegetables sometimes; some may lack flavour but canned vegetables such as carrots in plain brine add cheerful interest to well-flavoured but perhaps seamy-looking fresh vegetables.

Lastly, remember that having less than perfect vegetables is infinitely better than eating most stodgy starchy foods, and nearly as cheap. So don't ignore or throw out elderly less attractive vegetables. Cook them in ways which mask their coarse, tough texture yet make full use of the good food value they still offer. There are a few recipes for them in this chapter. You probably already know a good many others.

Sausage and Apple Dumplings, page 180 *(British Sausage Bureau)*

SALADS

—◆◆—

Spring and summer salads can be both beautiful and fragrant, certainly if home-grown. They should look so interesting, so crisp and vital, that they command attention instantly. There is no excuse for anyone, certainly not for a gardener, offering or eating the anonymous, conventional limp jumble served by restaurants as a side salad. We perpetuate this sad sort of salad for two reasons. First we think of a salad as a meal-making 'soft option'. No set recipe or stove-work is needed; and a salad will do as a side dish with any savoury food if we can't think of a better, or haven't time to cook properly. We don't expect or require it to have a personality. Second, because a salad is not cooked, as a rule, it doesn't occur to most of us that it *can* vary much.

In fact, a good salad has far more personality than most cooked vegetables; but it isn't easy to make. The flavours and scents of young, raw leafy vegetables are either very delicate or slightly tart, and are always subtle, so they must be carefully chosen to mix well with each other and with other foods, yet not be overwhelmed. Their firm shapes take longer to trim evenly than vegetables chopped up for cooking, and they need careful arranging to show up well in the dish. The effort is always worthwhile. A herb-scented fresh summer salad, whether conventional or a new variation, is hard to beat.

In making summer salads, anyone with a garden or allotment, or even window-boxes of herbs, starts with a big advantage over people dependent on shops. Small really *is* beautiful when it comes to salad-making. Small young leaves from garden crops and the tips of a few newly picked herb sprigs make a better salad than twice that quantity of vegetables which have travelled from a commercial grower's beds.

The growing number of health-food shops helps the city dweller to some extent. At least their lettuces are not packed in plastic bags, although their choice is limited, and they cannot offer delicacies such as the country gardener's tiny crisp beet and dandelion tops, delicate thinnings or fresh young salad leaves with their own marked scent of freshness.

Country dwellers face the same problems as townees in making good winter salads. Suitable vegetables are few, need a good deal of preparation and may still taste slightly coarse when you've done it all. They haven't much eye-appeal either. Yet salads are even more valuable in winter than in summer. Without the same choice of raw fruits, we need even more the extra vitamins, minerals and crisp fibrous textures which raw vegetables offer. For this reason, I have concentrated mainly on salads using winter vegetables or ones available year round, and have hunted down some vivid salads which use colour in interesting ways. They will show you that even ordinary winter vegetables served raw need not be dull.

Making winter salads
Most winter roots and any coarse stems and leaves are best blanched for use in salads. If you blanch them in water, however, some of the vitamin value and the crispness which identifies salad vegetables is usually lost; so I often blanch my winter vegetables by marinating them lightly in lemon juice and sometimes a sprinkling of salt.

In this instance it is wise economy to use bottled, natural lemon juice. Fresh whole lemons are expensive, and since other fruit is scarce in winter you should use their full food value and flavour by eating the whole fruit. (Grate the rind for flavouring cakes; add a whole lemon cut in eighths when you cook Brussels sprouts or kale, instead of just sharpening the water with juice. It softens, and can be served with the other vegetables.)

It is certainly more economical to use bottled juice to get enough to make a marinade or to dip vegetables to prevent them discolouring — you have to squeeze a lot of lemons to get enough juice to dip, say, sliced Jerusalem artichokes for four people. As for the old method of rubbing the cut side of a lemon over each slice, it wastes a lot of time and seldom coats the food completely.

Marinating in lemon juice often saves making a separate dressing. Here is a marinade for salad celeriac which you can use as a dressing afterwards just by adding oil:
For 1 medium 'root', weighing about 1½lb/700g use 2 tsp (2½ tsp) salt and 4 tsp (5 tsp) lemon juice, with 2 tbsp (2½ tbsp) chopped fresh winter herbs including a very little squeezed garlic and some finely chopped parsley stalks if possible. Use a little dried thyme or marjoram if you have no window-sill winter herbs. Peel the celeriac and grate it coarsely into thick shreds. Toss it thoroughly with the salt, lemon juice and herbs and leave it, covered, overnight.

To use it as *Celeriac Salad* making 4 side-dish helpings, mix ¼ tsp (½ tsp) dry mustard with another tbsp (1¼ tbsp) chopped herbs.

[121]

Toss the celeriac with these in about 2 tbsp (2½ tbsp) walnut oil (if you can get it) or a home-made herb oil (page 148). Taste, and add extra salt and lemon juice if you wish.

You can use this recipe for kohlrabi, turnip or carrot, or even for blanched cubed cabbage stalk if not coarse and fibrous.

Some salad vegetables are blanched in salt alone: sliced cucumber, for instance, courgettes or aubergines. Sprinkle the slices or chunks with coarse salt, and leave them on a tilted plate for about 30 minutes. Drain off the liquid which has seeped out, then dress the vegetables with a vinaigrette sauce.

CABBAGE AND SEED SALAD *(Serves 4)*
Colour picture page 51.

8oz/200g hard white cabbage,
  finely shredded (2 cups)
2 stalks celery, chopped (1 cup)
1 carrot, coarsely grated
1 tsp dill seed (1¼ tsp)
1 tsp poppy seed (1¼ tsp)
¼ tsp dried marjoram (½ tsp)

4 tbsp plain yoghurt (5 tbsp)
2 tsp lemon juice (2½ tsp)
1–2 tsp white cider vinegar
  (1¼–2½ tsp)
small pinch of sugar
salt and pepper to taste

Mix the vegetables, seeds and marjoram in a bowl. Sharpen the yoghurt with the lemon juice and vinegar and season to taste with sugar, salt and pepper. Toss with the vegetables. Refrigerate for 1–2 hours before use.

BROCCOLI SALAD *(Serves 2–4)*
Colour picture page 51.

4–6 heads sprouting broccoli
  (6–8oz/150–200g)
salt and pepper
2fl oz/50ml lemon juice (¼ cup)
2fl oz/50ml olive oil (¼ cup)

¼ tsp paprika (½ tsp)
½ tsp honey (¾ tsp)
2 tsp grated shallot (1 tbsp)
1 hard-boiled egg yolk

Cut the broccoli into small florets. Boil in very little water for 10 minutes. Drain, season, and cool slightly. Mix together the lemon juice, oil, paprika, honey and shallot. Toss with the broccoli. Put in a bowl, cover, and refrigerate overnight. Sieve the egg yolk over the salad just before serving.

MUSHROOM AND WATERCRESS SALAD *(Serves 4–6)*

Just a summer salad, but so different from the standard green leaves that it is well worth including as a way of ringing the changes. Freshly torn young dandelion or spinach leaves are just as refreshingly sharp as watercress.

1lb/450g fresh small mushrooms
4oz/100g watercress leaves
1 tbsp chopped parsley (1¼ tbsp)
1 tbsp chopped chives (1¼ tbsp)
rind of 1 small lemon
(see method)

FOR THE DRESSING:
3 tbsp olive or other pure vegetable
oil (4 tbsp)
1 tbsp cider vinegar (1¼ tbsp)
salt and freshly ground black pepper,
to taste

Slice the mushrooms thinly, and mix with the watercress leaves and parsley. Cut the lemon rind into very thin slivers or 'straws'. Make the dressing by combining the ingredients in a jar with a screw-on top, closing it and shaking it vigorously.

Toss the mushrooms and leaves with enough dressing to moisten lightly. Put them in a bowl and sprinkle the chives and lemon rind on top. The green and yellow garnish looks lovely on the dark mushrooms.

CELERY AND APPLE SALAD *(Serves 4)*

8 thin stalks celery
4 tomatoes
salt and pepper
3 sharp dessert apples

juice of 1 large or 2 small lemons
1 tbsp chopped parsley (1¼ tbsp)
salad oil (optional)

Slice the celery and tomatoes thinly. Season both with salt and pepper. Core the apples, and cut into small dice. Toss the dice at once in the lemon juice, and drain; reserve the lemon juice. Mix the celery and apple dice, adding the parsley.

Sprinkle the tomato slices with the reserved lemon juice, then lay them in a circle on a flat platter. Pile the celery and apple mixture in the middle. Sprinkle with salad oil if you wish.

HARLEQUIN SALAD *(Serves 4)*

If you have only a few fresh salad vegetables, make the most of them to extend a delicatessen salad. Soft cheese and a cider-vinegar dressing give texture and lively flavour contrasts as well as balanced nutrients to this mineral-rich one.

1 medium fennel bulb
1 small onion
1 medium green pepper
2 firm ripe tomatoes
12 pimento-stuffed olives, sliced
2 tbsp chopped parsley (2½ tbsp)
4oz/100g piece of cooked ham
8oz/200g piece of salami
3oz/75g full-fat soft cheese or 1
  small packet Philadelphia soft
  cheese (6 tbsp)

FOR THE DRESSING:
3 tbsp French cider vinegar (4 tbsp)
4 tbsp pure groundnut oil (5 tbsp)
¼ tsp French mustard (½ tsp)
salt and pepper
1–3 drops Worcester sauce
½ tsp caster sugar (¾ tsp superfine
  sugar)
1 tbsp double cream (1¼ tbsp
  heavy cream)

FOR GARNISH:
1 bunch watercress

Remove the outer fennel leaves and root end, cut the bulb into small pieces. Skin the onion, and chop finely. Seed the pepper and cut into strips. Cut the tomatoes into small pieces. Mix in a bowl with the olives and parsley.

Cut the ham and half the salami in ½in/1cm dice and mix in. Keep remaining salami for the surrounding cheese cones.

Mix together all the dressing ingredients except the cream. Whisk this in last. Toss the salad in the dressing thoroughly, and leave to stand for 15 minutes.

[124]

Pile in the centre of a flat platter. Slice remaining salami thinly and roll into cones. Soften the cheese and fill the cones. Arrange them around the centre salad, alternately with sprigs of watercress.

SWEET PEPPER AND ONION SALAD *(Serves 4)*

2 sweet red peppers	*lemon juice as needed*
1 large mild onion	*6 tbsp natural yoghurt (8 tbsp)*
4in/10cm piece cucumber	*sprinkling of paprika*
salt and pepper	

Core and seed the peppers, and peel the onion. Do not peel the cucumber unless the skin is ridged and tough. Chop all these vegetables into small pieces and season them well. Mix enough lemon juice and seasoning into the yoghurt to give it a pleasant tang.

Chill both salad vegetables and yoghurt slightly. Toss them together lightly, and sprinkle with paprika just before serving.

JUNCTION SALAD *(Serves 4–6)*

4oz/100g wholemeal spaghetti	*4oz/100g cooked green peas (³/4 cup)*
salt	*2 tbsp French dressing (2¹/2 tbsp)*
2 firm tomatoes, about 2oz/50g	*2 tbsp tomato ketchup (2¹/2 tbsp)*
each	*white pepper*
1 green pepper	*lemon juice if needed*
2oz/50g pitted and chopped black	
olives (¹/4 cup)	

Break the spaghetti into short lengths. Boil it in lightly salted water until just tender; drain, rinse under a cold tap, then cool under a damp cloth.

Core, skin and seed the tomatoes and pepper, then chop the flesh. Put the tomato, pepper and olives into a bowl, together with the peas. Mix in the spaghetti. Chill briefly.

Mix the French dressing with the tomato ketchup and any salt, pepper or lemon juice needed to make a sharp, spicy mixture. Turn the salad into a serving bowl, and trickle the tinted dressing over it just before serving.

Note: To make this a hearty main-course salad, add 3 sliced cooked chipolata sausages with the peas, and sprinkle the salad with 2–3 crisply cooked, crumbled bacon rashers (strips) after trickling on the dressing.

JELLIED CROWN SALAD *(Serves 4–6)*

Colour picture page 51.

This jellied beetroot salad is ruby red, and the Russian salad and sliced stuffed olives look like gold jewels. If you double the quantities, it will make a handsome buffet party centrepiece.

2 small carrots, coarsely grated
1 small turnip, coarsely grated
3–4 tsp bottled lemon juice
   (4–5 tsp)
1 1/2 tbsp gelatine (1 1/2 tbsp)
7 1/2 fl oz/185ml cold water (scant
   1 cup)

2oz/50g raw beetroot, cut in pieces
1oz/25g bean sprouts
7 1/2 fl oz/185ml natural pineapple
   juice (scant 1 cup)
1 1/2 tsp honey or to taste (2 tsp)
Imperial Russian Salad (page 134)
4 green pimiento-stuffed olives

Soak the carrot and turnip in the lemon juice for 2–3 hours. Stir the gelatine into the water in a saucepan, place over very low heat and leave to melt, stirring occasionally.

Put all the vegetables, the lemon juice and the pineapple juice in a food processor or blender, and process until the juice is crimson; if the machine is small, process in batches. Stop the machine before the vegetables are reduced to a purée. Stir the vegetables into the gelatine mixture with honey to taste.

Turn into a 1 1/4 pt/650ml ring mould and chill until set. Turn out onto a serving plate. Fill the jelly ring with Imperial Russian Salad, and garnish with sliced stuffed olives.

BEETROOT.

'SHORT' COOKING
(STIR-FRYING — STEAMING)

—◆◇—

'Short' cooking means cooking briefly to conserve as many vitamins as possible. In the case of vegetables, there are several ways of doing it. For instance you can blanch the vegetables well and eat them while they are still crisp, barely par-boiled. Alternatively, you can sauté them; this seals the surfaces, preventing vitamin loss, while the frying oil's heat does the cooking. If you shred them or slice them thinly, they cook by this stir-frying method so fast that vitamin loss from the shredded surfaces is stopped almost before it begins.

Stir-frying is one style of what the Japanese call nabé or one-pot cookery. Another style is to shred the vegetables (and meats or fish if you wish) as for stir-frying; but unstead of being sautéed in oil, they are dropped into a deep pot of boiling stock, those which take longest to cook going in first. Within a few moments, they can be lifted out with a slotted spoon, and arranged decoratively on the diners' plates. The stock, which already contains much of their goodness, can then be poured over them, or drunk separately. Both types of nabé cooking are easy and fun to do at the table.

Another cooking method which conserves vitamins and gives beautifully firm, fresh-tasting vegetables is steaming. Admittedly it takes longer, unless you cut the vegetables into tiny pieces; but it is a good way to conserve their vitamins because they never come into contact with water but are simply enveloped in the (hotter) steam which gently tenderises them.

Apart from their food value, the outstanding merit of all vegetables cooked in this way is that they are a pleasure to see and eat — their shapes are firm, their colour bright and their texture crisp. Make the most of this benefit and take the trouble, at least sometimes, to prepare them 'for show'. Trim baby carrots evenly; carve out potato balls with a vegetable baller instead of cubing them; gouge strips lengthways out of a cucumber's surface before slicing it. Decorative touches like these give you picture-book vegetables which are not only admired but are eaten avidly.

In this section, I have collected together recipes which use various methods of short-cooking vegetables to conserve their food value. Once you've tried them, you will find that you can very easily adapt them to make the most of other vegetables too.

[127]

GLAZED CARROTS (Serves 4)

1/4pt/125ml water (1/2 cup + 2 tbsp)
salt to taste
7–8 young carrots, coarsely shredded or cut into fine 'matchsticks'

2 tbsp butter (2 1/2 tbsp)
2 tsp light muscovado sugar or honey (2 1/2 tsp)
1 tsp lemon juice (1 1/4 tsp)
1/2 tsp chopped chives (3/4 tsp)
3/4 tsp chopped parsley (1 tsp)

Bring the water to the boil in a fairly large saucepan. Add all the ingredients except the herbs. Cover tightly, and cook over medium heat, shaking the pan, for 6–7 minutes or until all the water has evaporated.

Take the pan off the heat, and continue shaking it until the carrots are all coated with the glaze and are lightly steamed. Turn into a warmed serving dish, sprinkle with the herbs and serve at once.

CARROTS.

COURGETTE LEAVES (Serves 4)

Not quite a conventional stir-fry, but a dish of the same kind!

2 medium courgettes, about 4oz/100g each
2 large spring onion bulbs
1 egg
2 tbsp wholemeal flour (2 1/2 tbsp)
1 tbsp medium oatmeal (1 1/4 tbsp)
1 tbsp finely chopped parsley (1 1/4 tbsp)

1 tbsp milk (1 1/4 tbsp)
salt and pepper
2 tbsp frying oil (2 1/2–3 tbsp)
3 tbsp grated Swiss Gruyère cheese (4 tbsp) (optional)

Cut the courgettes diagonally into oval slices like leaves, about 1/4in/5mm thick. Dry in a cloth. Chop the spring onion bulbs finely. Whisk together the egg, flour, oatmeal, parsley and milk, and add the onion. Season well. Coat the courgette slices with the egg mixture.

Heat the oil, and fry the slices gently in batches, turning once, until patched with brown and beginning to soften. Remove with a slotted spoon to a warmed serving dish. Season. Sprinkle with the cheese if used, and serve while still hot, as the cheese begins to melt.

STEAMED CAULIFLOWER *(Serves 4–6)*

Cauliflower looks dramatic if you offer the compact whole head dressed with a tinted sauce as topping. It cooks surprisingly quickly.

1 medium cauliflower
2 tbsp butter (2½ tbsp)
salt and pepper

2 tbsp sieved hard-boiled egg yolk (2½ tbsp) or 1 tbsp finely snipped chives and 1 tbsp crumbled, crisply cooked bacon (1¼ tbsp)

Cut off the cauliflower stalk, but leave a few small leaves surrounding the head if possible. Cut a deep cross in the base of the stalk end. Put about 2in/5cm water in a large saucepan, and bring to steaming point. Put in the cauliflower head, stalk-side down, and cover tightly. Bring to the boil, lower the heat and simmer for 15–20 minutes, until just tender.

Put stalk-side down, in a warmed serving dish. Melt the butter and pour it over the cauliflower, season lightly, and sprinkle with egg yolk or chives and bacon.

AUBERGINE (EGGPLANT) ROUNDS *(Serves 4)*

1 medium aubergine (eggplant), about 11oz/275g
frying oil
salt and pepper

½ small onion, grated
3 tbsp finely grated mature Cheddar or Gouda cheese (4 tbsp)
cress leaves, finely chopped

Cut the peeled aubergine across into ½in/1cm rounds; brush both sides with oil and season. Lay on a greased flameproof serving plate and bake at 400°F (200°C), Gas 6 for 7 minutes. Turn over, cover with onion, and bake for 5 minutes longer.

Mix the cheese and cress leaves, sprinkle them on the slices, and either bake for 2 minutes longer or grill to melt the cheese.

LEEK SCRAMBLE *(Serves 2 as a main course or 4 as a side dish)*
Try this cooking method using shredded white cabbage.

1 large egg
1 tbsp cider vinegar (1¼ tbsp)
1 tbsp golden granulated sugar
  (1¼ tbsp)

6oz/150g white parts of leeks
  (3–4 leeks)
½ tsp salt (¾ tsp)
4 rindless streaky bacon rashers (4 strips)

Beat together the egg, vinegar and sugar. Slice the leeks finely and sprinkle with salt. Cut the bacon into small squares.

Fry the bacon slowly in a large frying pan, turning it until lightly browned all over. Add the leeks, cover with a plate, and 'steam' for 4 minutes over medium heat, shaking the pan from time to time. Pour the egg mixture over, and stir round quickly as the egg cooks. Serve at once.

SWEET-SOUR SALAD STIR-FRY *(Serves 4)*
This colourful sweet-sour vegetable medley makes a super-quick, stylish side dish for plain grilled chicken, turkey or gammon steaks. Arrange the vegetables on plates to look like flat flower posies, and cook them at the table if you have a spirit burner.

2 medium carrots
1 clove garlic
½ small piece stem ginger in syrup,
  drained
1 small or ½ large green or red
  pepper
1 medium onion
2 stalks celery

1 sharp dessert apple
3 tbsp white vinegar (4 tbsp)
2oz/50g golden granulated sugar
  (¼ cup)
1 tbsp medium sherry (1¼ tbsp)
1 tbsp water (1¼ tbsp)
2 tbsp frying oil (2½ tbsp)
salt and pepper

Scrape the carrots and cut them into thin 'matchsticks' about 1½in/ 3.5cm long. Blanch in boiling water for 2 minutes, then drain. Skin the garlic and chop finely with the ginger. Mix with the carrot and arrange on a plate.

Core, seed and slice the pepper. Skin the onion, halve it from stem to root end, and cut it into thin strips. Slice the celery thinly. Peel and core the apple and shred it on the coarse holes of a grater. Arrange all these on a second plate.

Heat the vinegar and sugar gently in a saucepan until the sugar melts, then stir in the sherry and water. Put into a small jug.

Bring the plates of raw vegetables, the vinegar syrup, oil and seasonings to the dinner table which should already be laid, with crispbreads or rolls, butter and so on at hand. You will need a spirit burner or gas ring which gives a high heat, a slotted metal spatula and a wooden spoon.

When everyone is assembled, heat the oil in a large deep frying-pan. Add the carrot, garlic and ginger, and stir over medium heat for 2 minutes. Add the remaining vegetables and apple and stir for another 2 minutes. Pour the vinegar syrup over the dish, and simmer for 2 minutes. Season to taste. Turn into a warmed dish and serve at once.

QUICK-SIMMERED MEDLEY *(Serves 4)*

This is based on a Japanese nabé dish called 'Temple of Jade'. You can vary the ingredients as you like, provided you keep the same proportions of green and root vegetables to meat or fish (2 parts vegetables to 1 part protein food). Whatever you choose, cut the raw ingredients into bite-sized pieces, and arrange them on plates as carefully as you would a flower bouquet.

8 spring onions
1 medium carrot, thinly sliced
2pt/1.1 litres well-flavoured white
 chicken or vegetable stock
 (5 cups)
1 tsp salt or as needed (1¼ tsp)
lemon juice or soy sauce to taste
1lb/450g round lettuce, cut across
 in 1½in/3.5cm strips

16 small mushroom caps, halved
2 courgettes, thinly sliced diagonally
1lb/450g white chicken or rabbit
 meat cut in ½in/1cm dice
2 rashers rindless back bacon, cut in
 small squares (2 strips)
hot cooked brown rice

Lay the table, and prepare the vegetables as for stir-frying. Chop the spring onion green and white parts separately, and put the chopped green in a small dish alone. Put the carrot in another dish by itself. Season the stock with salt and lemon juice or a very little soy sauce.

At the table, bring the stock to the boil in a large saucepan. Add some of the carrot, and cook gently for 2 minutes. Stir in about a quarter of each of the remaining ingredients except the green spring onion and cook for 5 minutes, skimming well. Add some of the green spring onion and simmer for 1 minute.

Scoop out portions of the mixture with a slotted spoon, and transfer to dinner plates with a few spoonfuls of the stock, to be eaten at once while hot, with brown rice. Add more raw ingredients to the stockpot to replace the ones served. Repeat until the whole dish has been cooked and eaten.

[131]

WHENEVER YOU WANT THEM

—◆◇◆—

Clever gardeners have ways of persuading their vegetable crops to produce before and after their proper season, and even year-round. As for storing vegetables — whether the peak season's crop or rarities — most gardening manuals and 'grow and use' gardeners' cook books describe in detail how to build an outdoor pit or stack and how to organise bulk storage in outhouse and cellar. A freezer is, of course, a superb friend to the vegetable-lover who has home-grown produce to spare and time to process it; for although no frozen vegetable has the fragrance of the fresh produce, home or commercially grown frozen vegetables are certainly better than none. Home-dried herbs are more rewarding than their bought counterparts if you have space for them. If not, Chapter 8 contains one or two other ways of preserving their flavour and aroma, while Chapter 10 includes pickles as a way of storing modest quantities of garden produce for use as flavourings and garnishes.

Although these are valuable cooking aids, many of us have neither space nor time to store vegetables for main-meal use; so when we cannot get the particular fresh vegetables we want or we need variety and new colour, we have to use canned or dried ones. There's usually nothing wrong with these nutritionally if you pick carefully. Choose the 'basics'. Go for cans which contain only one vegetable, and which have fewest additives listed on the label. Those packed in plain brine are best. Remember that chopped dried vegetables in cartons and packets are usually only intended to give flavour and colour, for which they are excellent; they have little nutritive value.

The main problem with the bulkier canned and freeze-dried vegetables is usually that they all taste bland and more or less the same. Making the most of them means giving them character. One good way to do this is to mix them with well-flavoured fresh vegetables; mixing two vegetables in the same dish gives each of them new interest, and you may come up with some intriguing texture and colour combinations. Another way is to give them unusual seasonings and garnishes. Good garnishing helps a lot — remember, too, that chopped parsley doesn't only look attractive, it has a mineral content, like chopped watercress or cress leaves. Give processed vegetables new textures; dry-fry sliced carrots for instance until they look 'rusty'.

[132]

Here are one or two ways to make the most of frozen or canned vegetables if you have to use them, and a 'freak' way in which even flat-dwellers can have one fresh vegetable year-round whenever they want it.

CASSEROLED BEANS AND TOMATOES *(Serves 4)*

12oz/300g cooked butter beans, or three 7¹/₂oz/213g cans butter or cannellini beans
1 tsp salt (1¹/₄ tsp)
grated rind of ¹/₂ lemon
2oz/50g butter (¹/₄ cup)
2 medium onions, chopped; or 4 tbsp (5 tbsp) dried sliced onions, soaked and drained

1 tsp crushed dried rosemary (1¹/₄ tsp)
4 medium tomatoes, or one 7¹/₂oz/ 213g can plum tomatoes, chopped
4oz/100g grated Cheddar cheese (1 cup)
1 tbsp chopped parsley (1¹/₄ tbsp)
melted butter
1 lemon, quartered

Put the beans and a good ¹/₄pt/125ml (¹/₂ cup + 2 tbsp) water into a saucepan (if using canned beans, use the liquid with them). Add the salt, bring to the boil and simmer for 4 minutes to heat through. Drain, and sprinkle with the lemon rind.

Melt the butter in a frying pan. Add the onions and rosemary and stir over low heat until the onions are soft and light gold. Mix with the beans.

Grease a deep 1³/₄pt/1 litre (4¹/₂ cups) oven-to-table casserole. Spread half the bean mixture evenly over the bottom. Cover with half the tomatoes, and sprinkle with half the cheese. Repeat the

[133]

layers once, adding the parsley to the top layer of cheese. Sprinkle with melted butter.

Bake at 375°F (190°C), Gas 5 for 20 minutes or until well heated through, with a golden crust. Serve with lemon quarters.

FRENCH BEANS SOUBISE *(Serves 4–6)*
Frozen vegetables take less time to cook than fresh ones, canned ones less time still. If you use 'preserved' vegetables to supplement a scanty fresh supply, add them part-way through the cooking time.

12oz/300g prepared fresh, or frozen and thawed, French beans; or one 15oz/425g can
2 tbsp butter (2½ tbsp)

12 spring onions (white bulbs), trimmed
juice of 1 small lemon
salt and pepper to taste
1 small clove garlic, crushed

Steam the beans in a strainer over simmering water until they are just tender (keep the water for stock). Meanwhile, melt half the butter in a pan, add the onions, toss well, then cover and simmer gently until the onions are tender.

Toss the beans, when cooked, with the remaining butter and the lemon juice, season well, and squeeze the garlic over them. Turn into a warmed serving dish and sprinkle with the onions.

IMPERIAL RUSSIAN SALAD *(Serves 4)*
Colour picture page 51.

8oz/227g pkt frozen mixed vegetables, thawed
½ tsp chopped fresh parsley (½ tsp)
1 tsp dried sliced onion, soaked and drained (1¼ tsp)
1½ tsp lemon juice (2 tsp)

¼ tsp Worcester sauce (½ tsp)
½ tsp turmeric (¾ tsp)
¼pt/125ml mayonnaise
salt and pepper
¼–½ tsp caster sugar (½–¾ tsp) (optional)

Blanch the mixed vegetables in boiling water if you wish. Drain and cool. Mix in the parsley and onion. Stir the lemon juice, Worcester sauce and turmeric into the mayonnaise. Season to taste, adding sugar if you wish. Mix with the vegetables.

Sausage, Leek and Cider Bake, page 181 *(British Sausage Bureau)*

SOFA MUSHROOMS *(Makes 5–10lb/2.3–4.5kg mushrooms)*

Whether you live in a flat, a terraced house in a city street or a country cottage, this 'recipe' will give you earthy-fresh mushrooms year-round at a third to a fifth of shop prices. The method was given to me by Chris Snook, a horticultural expert at a garden centre.

1 sofa
1–2 mushroom bags (obtainable
from good garden centres)

1 capillary wick and jam jar
1 mist spray

Take one large sofa. Position it so as to minimise traffic behind it, and in this quiet space, place a mushroom bag. Open it as directed, and scatter the casing material onto the compost. Lead a capillary wick to it from an adjacent jam jar of water.

The mushrooms start growing from the spawn at a temperature around 60°F/16°C when the casing is moist. *Daily* examination of the bag by peering over the sofa top is essential; so is watering with the mist spray. If the casing material dries out, the mushrooms will die.

One mushroom bag will produce up to 10lb/4.5kg mushrooms in several flushes. You can pick them while still button size or let them grow as large as coffee-cup saucers for stuffing. The colour will vary from white to pale fawn, depending wholly on how much light they are exposed to. An average bag will go on producing mushrooms for 2–3 months; start a new bag when the one in action seems near the end of its life.

Remember that the contents of the finished bag make an excellent mulch for the garden or for window-sill pots — and may even give you a last crop of mushrooms.

Apart from being much cheaper and always at hand, the flavour of sofa mushrooms is incomparably better than that of shop-bought ones.

Devilled Drumsticks with Cream Sauce, page 184 *(Colman's Mustard)*

USING LESS THAN PERFECT VEGETABLES

—◆◆—

POTATO CAKES *(Makes 8 'cakes')*
Perhaps the most versatile way you can use potatoes, especially leftovers! Offer them topped with butter as a side dish, or with bacon for breakfast. Make them the basis of a main supper dish, with a rich meat sauce and chopped sausage; or sandwich them with a spicy filling — this way, they'll even do duty as hamburger 'buns'.

1lb/450g mashed potato
2 tbsp flour (2½ tbsp)
salt and pepper
fat for frying

IMPROVED POTATO-
STEAMER.

Mix the potato and flour, and season well. Roll out to ¼–½in/ 5mm–1cm thick on a floured surface. Fry in a very little hot fat for 3–4 minutes on each side, until lightly browned.

BAKED CARROT CASSEROLE *(Serves 6)*
A good way to use elderly carrots! Serve this slightly sweet-sour casserole with baked gammon or frankfurters; or with steamed, buttered cabbage mixed with caraway seeds, and cubed mild cheese.

6oz/150g Toasted Farmhouse Bran
  (3 cups)
12oz/300g grated carrots
2 tsp chopped parsley (2½ tsp)
2 eggs, lightly beaten
½pt/250ml milk (1¼ cups)

1 tsp vinegar (1¼ tsp)
1 tsp salt (1¼ tsp)
good pinch of ground black pepper
1½oz/35g butter or margarine,
  melted (3 tbsp)
extra melted butter for sprinkling

Crush the breakfast cereal to fine even crumbs. Reserve 1oz/25g, then mix the remaining crumbs with all the other ingredients, except the butter for sprinkling. Turn into a greased 1¾pt/1 litre (4½ cups) casserole or baking dish. Scatter the reserved crumbs on top. Sprinkle with butter.
    Bake at 350°F (180°C), Gas 4 for 45 minutes. Serve hot.

SPRINGTIME LOAF *(Serves 6)*

This looks spring-like with its flecks of orange among the green and gold of leaves and egg. Yet it makes a substantial hot supper or cold packed meal out of leftovers and single, lorn vegetables.

No slimmer could feel deprived with a slice of this firm loaf inside him, yet it is largely fat-free protein and vegetables.

2 *small carrots*
1 *medium-sized onion*
1 *tbsp frying oil (1¼ tbsp)*
12oz/300g *finely chopped, cooked*
  spring greens (can be leftovers)
  (2 cups)
½ *tsp fresh or dried chopped*
  thyme (¾ tsp)

½ *tsp fresh or dried chopped*
  marjoram (¾ tsp)
6 *eggs*
½ *tsp salt (¾ tsp)*
butter, flaked, for greasing and
  topping

Grate the carrots and onion coarsely in a food processor or mill. Heat the oil, and stir the grated vegetables in it for 2 minutes. Turn them into a bowl, and mix in the spring greens and herbs. Beat the eggs lightly, and mix in thoroughly. Season.

Grease or line a 7½in x 3½in x 2¼in/185mm x 90mm x 50mm loaf tin; turn in the mixture and sprinkle with flaked butter. Bake at 350°F (180°C), Gas 4 for 40 minutes. Serve hot; or cool in the tin, loosen and turn out for slicing.

Note: The loaf shrinks as it cools.

RATATOUILLE *(Serves 4–6)*

Ratatouille is good hot or cold, and freezes perfectly, ready for whenever you need it. Thaw at room temperature for 3 hours. Serve as a first course, as a side dish with red meat, or as a salad lunch topped with crumbled cheese such as Boursin, Féta or Chèvre. *Colour picture page 52.*

3 *medium aubergines*
salt
2 *large onions*
1 *clove garlic*
1 *green pepper*
2–3 *courgettes*

4–6 *tomatoes*
3oz/75g *margarine (⅓ cup)*
pepper
2 *bay leaves*
chopped parsley

Slice the aubergines thinly and cover with salt. Leave for 30 minutes. Meanwhile skin, halve and slice the onions; crush the garlic; seed and slice the pepper; slice the courgettes thinly; skin and quarter the tomatoes.

[139]

Melt the margarine in a large deep frying pan or saucepan. Add the onions, garlic and pepper; cover and cook over low heat for 5 minutes without letting them brown. Drain the aubergine, and add with all the other ingredients except the parsley. Cover and cook gently for 30 minutes. Remove the bay leaves.

To serve hot, put in a serving dish and sprinkle with chopped parsley.

To freeze: Put the vegetables in a rigid container without the parsley. Level, then cover and fast-freeze. When wanted, thaw at room temperature for 3 hours. Reheat gently, then garnish.

Vegetable Purées
Using less-than-beautiful vegetables in purées is a wonderful way to make the best of them. The number of possible vegetable combinations is almost endless: so you can experiment, besides trying the classic ones, using a single leftover or 'ugly duckling' vegetable or a few mixed ones. They'll look good, and almost certainly taste good.

Serving a vegetable purée as a side dish with meat is one of the ideas of the modern French 'cuisine minceur', and it is a great one. Since the purée is not thickened with a starchy sauce, its natural flavours are undiminished (it will appeal to slimmers too). Its smooth texture complements the rougher textures of roast or grilled meat or — better still — poultry; and in the age of the food processor and blender it is easy for anyone who possesses either to make the purée velvet-smooth.

Purées made with pulses or nuts, or containing a proportion of starchy vegetables, need no extra thickening at all. Watery fresh vegetables such as spinach must either be 'dried out' with a little butter in the pan, or have egg or cream added. The choice is yours.

PARSLEY CHAMP *(Serves 4)*
Champ is a traditional Irish Friday night supper dish. It is made by pounding or puréeing potatoes with another vegetable which has been cooked in milk. Each helping is served with a big knob of butter in the middle. The champ is eaten from the outside with a spoon which you dip into the melting butter.

1 1/2lb/700g floury potatoes	*salt and pepper*
3 tbsp chopped parsley (3 1/2 tbsp)	*4 knobs butter*
1/4pt/125ml milk or as needed	
(1/2 cup + 2 tbsp)	

Boil the potatoes in their skins in salted water until tender. Boil the parsley in the milk for 3 minutes. Peel and pound the potatoes or mash them, adding the parsley and milk gradually while processing. Add any extra hot milk needed to make the potatoes smooth and creamy. Season well. Serve each helping with a knob of butter.

Variation:

Make spring onion champ, using 6 spring onions and ½pt/250ml (1¼ cups) milk.

Chop the green and white parts of the onions, sprinkle with ½ tsp (¾ tsp) salt and pour boiling water over them. Drain. Simmer in the milk for 20 minutes, then add to the potatoes as above.

PARSLEY.

PARSNIP PURÉE *(Serves 4–6)*

The sweetish flavour of parsnips sometimes makes them unpopular; but mixed with potato and well seasoned, their sweetness is muted. The fibrous texture of older ones, left too long in the ground, is also coped with if they are puréed.

1lb/450g cooked and peeled parsnips
12oz/300g peeled, boiled potatoes
1 tbsp softened butter (1¼ tbsp)
2–4 tbsp milk to give consistency desired (2½–5 tbsp)

salt and ground black pepper to taste
good pinch of grated nutmeg
1 tbsp double cream (1¼ tbsp heavy cream) (optional)
4–6 spoonfuls unsalted butter

Cut the cooked vegetables into small pieces. Sieve them, or purée in a food processor until smooth; in either case, mix in the butter and milk while processing. Taste, add seasoning and nutmeg, and stir in cream if used. Heat very gently without boiling.

Grind a little extra black pepper over the top of the purée. Serve each helping with a spoonful of butter in the middle.

[141]

8

GOOD VALUE HERB PRODUCTS

—◆◇◆—

Herbs are the liveliest plants we grow and use. Their flavour may be subtle or vibrant, dominant or insidious; but from the nature of herbs it is always there, underpinning or rounding out any other flavours. Nine-tenths of our savoury dishes are created by the herbs we use in them. Proof lies in any standard cookery book. Riffle through its pages from Soups to Savouries and see how many dishes you can find *without* herbs: few indeed, especially if you include chives, seed and stem fennel, fresh ginger, mustard seed and garlic!

Some herbs provide nutrients or remedies as well as flavour and aroma; but even without these, their taste and scent make herbs indispensable. Good looks, flavour and variety in food encourage digestion; and chopped parsley, a hint of garlic, a pattern of bay leaves on a terrine or the savour of fresh basil on tomatoes, invigorate our eating.

Our forebears knew the value of herbs. Country children were sent out in early spring to search the hedgerows and woodland for the first herbs, to add new flavour to the standard one-pot dinner boiled in a cauldron; in particular to the solid 'pudden' eaten first, to take the edge off eager appetites! Later in the year, no table was complete without its herb salad or dishes of stewing and chewing herbs. There is evidence for it in Greek and Roman meals.

[142]

Fresh and home-dried herbs have an impact which bought, dried ones cannot match. Mass drying seems to diminish the herbs, and it is impossible to tell how long the bought ones have been in the packet or carton. Even a flat-dweller will find it worthwhile to grow a few herbs in pots (perhaps instead of having bulbs in a bowl or cut flowers). Any food he (or she) offers will not only be improved but will carry a personal signature.

Since so many of our dishes depend on herbs for their character, you will find recipes which use herbs in interesting ways in most good cookery books. So here, I am just giving you one or two ways of preserving fresh herbs which make them basic ingredients for other cooking. A flat-dweller often has no suitable space to dry his own, but need not be deprived of them for that reason; there are other methods.

For centuries, French cooks have made herb vinegars, herb oils and herb butters, to dress and garnish their dishes. A few of these are now commercially made. I only wish there were more. Pending that day, let's make our own. It is easier than drying herbs in fact, and more decorative. I have a row of bottles, each holding its graceful patterned herb spray, along my window-sill. They give me much pleasure, and also I find them excellent token gifts to take to friends.

LEMON THYME.

DRYING HERBS

For people who have herbs in quantity and space to store them, drying is the best all-purpose way to preserve most of them. Herbs can be frozen but I do not find it satisfactory: my herbs all tend to blacken and lose their flavour, they tend to cross-flavour other foods in the freezer, and they sometimes give a musty taste to frozen dishes.

[143]

One can, however, dry any herbs except borage, chervil, chives and lemon balm. Remember that herbs keep their colour and aroma best if dried out of direct sunlight. Dry them standing upright in a jar or tall glass if you have only a few; dry big bunches by tying the stems together with string and hanging the herbs upside down from an outhouse or attic ceiling (not a room in use, or the garage). Give them plenty of time to dry if you want to store the leaves in jars for cooking. You can even give them a few minutes in the oven at plate-warming heat when you have stripped the stems. Be careful, though; don't risk drying out their essential oils and losing their flavour, scent and value.

I myself do not grow enough fresh herbs to supply dry ones for the whole winter, so I buy my dried ones and replace the supply often; I put my few precious fresh ones into vinegar or oil as a decorative way of storing them and making the most of what they offer.

MARJORAM.

HERB VINEGARS

Vinegar has been made for as long as wine, or longer. It is at least 3,000 years old, although it only seems to have arrived in western Europe in the Middle Ages. Spiced as well as herb vinegars were popular then; people's tastes were trained to be more robust than ours by having to eat heavily salted and spiced foods.

Five basic types of vinegar are sold in our stores. Distilled vinegar is the strongest. Although it cleans paint off copper or brass splendidly, this is hardly a recommendation for using it as a steeping medium for herbs. Certainly it wilts salad leaves almost at once if you use it in a salad dressing. Keep it for its proper purpose as a cleaning medium, or use a drop or two in curried and other spicy meat dishes.

Malt vinegar is a straight byproduct of the barley used for brewing. It used to be called ale vinegar or alegar, and has always been the kind most used by the English. It has, however, a distinct 'bite' and is not therefore ideal for making aromatic vinegars.

Red wine and white wine vinegars are the types which are, not surprisingly, used most by the French for all purposes including making aromatic vinegars. Red wine vinegar is the most popular in France, although our tastes generally prefer vinegar based on white wine. The best French wine vinegar of either type is Orleans vinegar; it is fresh and sharp on the palate, with a hint of the wine it is made from. If you have a fairly acute sense of taste, you will enjoy 'marrying' the flavour of a wine vinegar with different herbs, to create a whole range of subtle flavours.

Probably you will prefer wine vinegars to cider vinegar, but although not officially proven, quite strong evidence suggests that cider vinegar is markedly more health-promoting than other vinegars; it is said to prevent or at least ameliorate common colds and bronchitis, for instance. Since its flavour, although sharp, is not biting, it is quite suitable for making your herb vinegars; so I suggest you use it, and gain advantage from any health-giving properties it may have as well.

Always use a so-called white vinegar for herb vinegars — or one as near transparent as you can get it. The leafy sprays of the herbs, which identify them as well as looking beautiful, do not show up in red vinegar.

[145]

The basic method of making any herb vinegar is the same. Pick fairly mature sprays, leaves or flowers on a dry sunny day. Half-dry them for 4–5 days (elder flowers for 10–12 days) to get a more concentrated flavour quickly if you wish. Personally I put mine in vinegar fresh, for their looks and for convenience, and leave them in the vinegar twice as long as usual.

Have ready wide-necked bottles or jars with vinegar-proof lids or stoppers. Jars which have held pickles are excellent. Fill the clean jars with vinegar. Put a herb spray or two in each: one 4in/10cm spray per ½pt/250ml (1¼ cups) should be enough. Seal the bottles or jars securely. Leave in a cool dry place for 12–20 days, depending on how strongly flavoured your herb is. Strain the vinegar into a clean bottle, seal with a vinegar-proof stopper, label with name and date, and store.

MINT.

MINT VINEGAR *(Makes 1pt/500ml [2½ cups])*
The Romans called mint vinegar *posca acetum* and drank it with water as a refresher.

1pt/500ml white wine or cider   *2 sprays mint (any type)*
  vinegar (2½ cups)   *2–3 tsp caster sugar (2½–4 tsp)*

Pour the vinegar into a wide-necked clear glass bottle or jar with a secure, vinegar-proof lid or stopper. Put in the mint sprays and sugar, and stopper securely. Leave in a cool place for 2–3 weeks. Strain the vinegar into a clean bottle or jar, seal, label and store.

Mint vinegar has many uses. In particular: add a few drops to a cold punch or fruit cup; use it for seasoning cold green-bean or cucumber salad; season melted butter with it, and pour a little over young cooked hot peas, courgettes or broad beans; sprinkle it, with melted butter, over cooked, hot fennel or plainly grilled white fish.

[146]

TARRAGON VINEGAR *(Makes 1pt/500ml [2¹/2 cups])*

1pt/500ml white wine or cider   *two 4in/10cm sprays tarragon*
  vinegar (2¹/2 cups)

Put the vinegar and tarragon into a wide-necked bottle or jar with a vinegar-proof lid or stopper. Seal securely. Leave in a cool place for 2–3 weeks. Take out the sprays and re-seal, label and store.

Most salad dressing are improved by being made with tarragon vinegar. Use it, too, for any cold chicken dish which is dressed with mayonnaise.

Variation:
Make Basil Vinegar in exactly the same way. It is excellent sprinkled over grilled sliced tomatoes or a tomato salad.

TARRAGON.

ROSE VINEGAR *(Makes 1pt/500ml [2¹/2 cups])*

1pt/500ml white wine or cider   *a few drops of rose essence*
  vinegar (2¹/2 cups)   *petals of 1–2 dark-red, scented roses*

Modern roses have so little real scent compared with the old-fashioned ones that we can justifiably 'help' our vinegar with a little essence to get nearer to the old-style kind. Add the essence and petals to the vinegar and seal securely with a vinegar-proof seal. Leave in a cool place for 2–3 weeks. The petals will give up their colour and look like wet tissue-paper, but the vinegar should be a lovely pink. Strain, bottle and seal with a vinegar-proof stopper like other vinegars.

Use a drop or two to sharpen bland stewed fruits (where you would normally use lemon juice). You can also use it to scent and sharpen the water in finger-bowls at the dinner-table if you ever use them; they are quite a sensible idea if you serve fresh grapes or other fresh fruit instead of a pudding.

[147]

HERB OILS

—◆◇◆—

Herb oils are made simply by steeping the herbs in pure oil, but unlike vinegars they may develop off-flavours over a period, so it is wise only to make a small quantity of any particular kind, and to use it reasonably soon. Also flavoured oil does not react kindly to being exposed to air, so you do not want to have a big bottle which you must open and close several times before it is used up. For this reason, completely fill the jars in which you prepare herb oils; do not leave any headspace. If necessary, adapt the quantities of leaves and oil in the recipes below.

Use a pure unflavoured vegetable oil such as sunflower, corn or groundnut oil. Don't use olive oil, still less the rare but beautiful walnut oil. They are already flavoured oils, which give and gain nothing if herb flavourings are added.

ROSEMARY OIL *(Makes 1/2pt/250ml [1 1/4 cups])*

5 tsp bruised fresh rosemary leaves   *1/2pt/250ml pure vegetable oil*
  (6 tsp)   *(1 1/4 cups)*

Tip the leaves into a wide-necked jar with a very tight-fitting flat-topped lid. Pour in the oil. Close securely. Leave in a cool dark place for 2 weeks. For the first 4 days, invert the jar daily, then leave it right way up. Strain the oil into a clean container with a tight stopper, for use at once or later.

Sprinkle on pork or lamb chops before grilling them, on a broad bean salad or hot cooked haricot beans; also good for sprinkling on Mozzarella or Féta cheese when using them in a salad or pizza.

GARLIC OIL *(Makes 1/2pt/250ml [1 1/4 cups])*

3–4 cloves garlic, to taste
1/2pt/250ml pure vegetable oil (1 1/4 cups)

Remove any loose papery skin from the garlic cloves but not the close-fitting skin. Put them in a jar with a very tight-fitting flat-topped lid, pour in the oil and seal securely. Leave in a cool dark place for 2 weeks. For the first 4 days, invert the jar daily, then leave it right way up. Strain the oil into a clean container with a tight stopper, for use at once or later.

[148]

Garlic oil makes superb salad dressings. It is good sprinkled on sprigs of raw vegetables served as snacks or on hors d'oeuvres. Sprinkle the oil likewise over freshly boiled or baked potatoes, potato or tomato salad, hot white beans or pasta. Fry small cubes or triangles of bread in garlic oil, and use them to garnish any well-flavoured meat dish, or mix them into a salad.

SHALOT.

HERB BUTTERS

——◆◇◆——

Herb butters do not last as long as herb vinegars, but they are a super way to enjoy the freshness and flavour of your herbs for some time after their season has passed.

Most mild herb butters will freeze satisfactorily for 2–3 months. Make all herb butters in the same way. Chop the herbs finely, and work them into the softened butter with the back of a spoon. Use unsalted butter if possible, and add salt to taste after making. Shape the butter into a roll, close-wrap in polythene or greaseproof paper and seal with tape. Then freeze. Use while still well chilled. Cut slices as pats, or scrape off long curls with a continental cheese slicer, for topping savouries.

For more immediate use, package your herb butter as for freezing, and chill it, or put it in a salad pot in the refrigerator. Use refrigerated herb butters within 2 weeks. Soften and use for sandwiches or spread thinly on biscuits for serving with cheese or soup. Use pats for garnishing grilled steaks or fish, curls for garnishing cold meats and poultry.

[149]

TARRAGON BUTTER *(Makes about 2oz/50g [¹/4 cup] butter)*

1¹/2–2 tsp tarragon leaves   2oz/50g butter, softened (¹/4 cup)
  (2–2¹/2 tsp)   salt and white pepper

The old way:
Pick tarragon leaves, scald and dry them and, when cold, pound them in a mortar with butter, a little salt and white pepper. Rub through a hair sieve and keep in a cool place.

The new way:
Chop the leaves finely in a food processor or blender, adding the butter while processing. Blend until quite smooth. Season to taste.

BEURRE NOIR *(Makes about ¹/4pt/125ml [¹/2 cup + 2 tbsp] to cover a dish for 4 people)*

4oz/100g butter (¹/2 cup)   2 tbsp cider or wine vinegar
1 tbsp chopped parsley (1¹/4 tbsp)   (2¹/2 tbsp)

Melt the butter in a small pan and heat gently until light brown (not very dark as the butter will then taste burnt). Cool it slightly, and stir in the parsley and vinegar. Pour over a hot fish dish or brains just before serving.

Note: 1 tbsp (1¹/4 tbsp) chopped capers or gherkins can be added with the vinegar and parsley.

BASIL.

MAÎTRE D'HÔTEL BUTTER *(Makes 2oz/50g [¹/4 cup])*

2oz/50g butter (¹/4 cup)   a squeeze of lemon juice
1–2 tbsp parsley (1¹/4–2¹/2 tbsp)   salt and cayenne pepper to taste
a few finely snipped chives

Soften and cream the butter, then work in the parsley, chives if used, lemon juice and seasoning. Shape into an oblong or roll, wrap in greaseproof paper or foil, and chill. When firm, cut into small pats, and put on top of grilled fish or steaks just before serving.

CANAPÉ BUTTER *(Makes 5oz/125g [¹/₂ cup + 2 tbsp])*
Use chilled pats of this tinted butter on hamburgers (steaks if you
can afford them); or spread on canapés or open sandwiches. It is not
suitable for piping.

6 large parsley sprigs (leaves only)   *1 tsp corn oil (1¹/₄ tsp)*
1 hard-boiled egg yolk   *pinch of salt (optional)*
12 capers, drained   *4oz/100g unsalted butter (¹/₂ cup)*
pinch of powdered mace
1 tsp Tarragon Vinegar (page 147)
*   (1¹/₄ tsp)*

Rinse the parsley leaves and put into a food processor. Add the egg
yolk, capers, mace, vinegar, oil and salt if used. Process until
chopped to a 'mush'. Still processing, add the butter gradually, and
stop the machine as soon as it is blended in; the mixture should be
pale green with dark flecks.

Chill in a covered foil container until needed.

MACE.

Apart from the four classic herb butters given as recipes in this
section, here are some good butter-herb combinations. With 2oz/
50g (¼ cup) butter use:

1 clove garlic, squeezed, for *Garlic Butter*
good pinch each of fresh chopped thyme and parsley for *Herb*
    Butter
2 tbsp (2½ tbsp) finely chopped watercress leaves for *Montpelier* or
    Watercress Butter
½oz/15g shallot, squeezed (1 tbsp) for *Shallot Butter*
2 tsp finely chopped chives (2½ tsp) for *Chive Butter*
1½ tbsp very finely chopped mint leaves (2 tbsp) for *Mint Butter.*

USING YOUR HERB PRODUCTS

—◆◆—

Here are a few recipes using herb vinegars and oils.

TOMATO AND THYME SOUP *(Serves 4)*
No one would call tomato soup out of the ordinary; yet just a tea-spoon of fresh thyme and a few drops of thyme vinegar give it speciality status.
Colour picture page 34

¹/₂oz/15g margarine (1 tbsp)
1 onion, finely chopped
one 15oz/425g can whole
  tomatoes, crushed and strained
¹/₂pt/250ml chicken stock (can be
  from cube) (1¹/₄ cups)

1–3 drops each Worcester sauce and
  thyme vinegar
1 tsp finely chopped fresh thyme
  (1¹/₄ tsp)
grated rind of 1 orange

Melt the margarine, and simmer the onion in it until soft. Add the remaining ingredients, and continue simmering for 10–15 minutes. Serve with hot Herb Bread (page 84).

MINTED MELON AND CUCUMBER *(Serves 4)*
Don't be put off buying a melon if you won't be able to eat it all at one meal. The rest will make this delicious 'starter' or side-dish.

¹/₂ small honeydew melon
¹/₂ medium cucumber
1 large orange
6–8 fresh mint leaves

pinch of salt
good pinch of sugar
2 tsp mint vinegar or to taste (2¹/₂ tsp)
2 tsp water (2¹/₂ tsp)

Cut the melon flesh into small balls with a potato baller. Cut the (unpeeled) cucumber into chunks the same size as the melon balls. Peel the orange, and cut the flesh into segments free of skin and pith. Cut the segments in half across. Mix all the fruits. Chop the mint leaves finely and mix them in.

Mix together the salt, sugar, vinegar and water to make a tangy but not sharp mixture. Sprinkle over the fruit and mint. Chill well before serving.

HERB AND PORK MEAT PÂTÉ *(Serves 6–8)*

This pâté is usually served hot, in its pie dish, as a main course for supper. Fresh herbs make even vacuum-packed processed meat fragrant and delicious — a point to remember for bank holiday weekends.

*10–12 large back bacon rashers
(strips)
12oz/300g piece or three 4oz/113g
pkts pork luncheon meat or
chopped ham and pork
12oz/300g cooked Swiss chard or
spinach leaves, squeezed as
dry as possible
2–3 sprigs fresh parsley, chopped*

*2 sprigs each fresh basil and thyme
or ½ tsp each dried basil and
thyme (¾ tsp each)
½ tsp salt (¾ tsp)
1 tsp thyme or basil vinegar (1¼ tsp)
1 medium onion
1 large clove garlic
salt and pepper
2 (size 3) eggs*

Grease a 2¼pt/1.2 litre (2¾ pt) pie dish and spread 2 bacon rashers (strips) flat on the bottom. Chop 2 of the remaining rashers with the pork luncheon meat or ham and pork. Process them until pasty in a food processor or blender. Chop 2 more rashers into fairly small pieces and mix them into the paste for a contrasting texture.

Chop the chard or spinach leaves with any fresh herbs used; mix in the salt and vinegar and any dried herbs used. Chop the onion, not too finely, and squeeze the garlic over it.

Mix the garlicky onion, and then the leaves, into the meat mixture. Season well. Add the eggs and mix very thoroughly to distribute all the ingredients evenly. Turn the mixture into the prepared

[153]

pie dish, and level the surface. Cut the remaining bacon rashers in half and lay on top.

Cover the pie dish securely with greased foil. Stand it in a baking tin with enough hot water to come half-way up its sides. Bake at 350°F (180°C), Gas 4 for 50 minutes. Uncover for the last 10 minutes to let the bacon dry off and brown.

Blot off any excess free fat, and serve at once from the dish. Broad beans or carrots make a good vegetable with the pâté.

SALAD-STUFFED ROLLS *(Serves 4–8)*

A ready-to-eat salad meal for many occasions. Ideal for a teenagers' buffet party, or to leave as a refrigerator help-yourself meal for children who get home from school before you do. The dressing is named after the garlic-flavoured piece of toast or bread called a *chapon*, which French cooks sometimes put in salads to flavour them.

4 round crisp dinner rolls	CHAPON SALAD DRESSING:
1 small carrot	*1 tbsp garlic oil (1¼ tbsp)*
2–3 young crisp lettuce leaves	*2 tsp cider vinegar (1 tbsp)*
½ stalk celery	*1–2 tsp lemon juice or to taste (1¼ tsp*
1 large spring onion, green and	*or to taste)*
white parts	*½ tsp salt (¾ tsp)*
1 hard-boiled egg	*pinch of pepper*
4oz/100g cooked brown rice	*¼ tsp dry mustard (¼ tsp)*
(²/₃ cup)	
2oz/50g cooked butter beans	
(¹/₃ cup)	

Slit the rolls across into two equal halves. Scoop out all the crumb from both halves, leaving 8 crusty 'bowls'.

Grate the carrot. Shred the lettuce leaves finely. Slice the celery and spring onion thinly. Chop the egg. Mix all these with the rice and beans.

Shake all the dressing ingredients together in a screw-topped jar. Pour it over the salad. Leave, covered, for 15 minutes.

With the back of a spoon, mash down the rice and beans until pasty enough to bind the vegetables. Spoon into the dinner roll bowls.

To transport the salads for a picnic or packed meal, or to store them in the refrigerator, stick the two cut sides of each roll together, re-shaping them. Push a knife blade through the original slit to open them for serving.

[154]

TARRAGON MAYONNAISE *(Makes about ¹/₄pt/125ml [¹/₂ cup + 2 tbsp])*

1 large egg
pinch each of sea salt and freshly ground black pepper

1 tbsp tarragon vinegar (1¹/₄ tbsp)
¹/₄ tsp honey (¹/₂ tsp) (optional)
4fl oz/100ml oil (¹/₂ cup)

Put the egg, seasonings, vinegar and honey, if used, in an electric blender. Process for 5 seconds. With the motor still running, trickle in the oil, a few drops at a time, until the mayonnaise thickens.

Variation:
Use 2 yolks instead of a whole egg; yolks alone make slightly thinner mayonnaise. Whisk one egg white until stiff, and fold it into the mayonnaise just before serving, to make it fluffy.

Use with fish or chicken salad, or mix a spoonful with hot green peas instead of the usual mint and melted butter.

HERB AND EGG DIP *(Makes a good ³/₄pt/375ml [2 cups])*
Use raw carrot, celery sticks and blanched cauliflower sprigs as 'dunkers' with this fragrant dip.

4 hard-boiled eggs, finely chopped
2oz/50g cooked white butter or haricot beans, puréed
¹/₂ tsp chopped fresh mixed herbs as available (³/₄ tsp)

2 tbsp lemon juice (2¹/₂ tbsp)
1 tsp finely grated onion (1¹/₄ tsp)
4fl oz/100ml Tarragon Mayonnaise (above) (¹/₂ cup)
salt and pepper

Mix all the ingredients until well blended, and chill for at least 1 hour before use.

SAGE.

9

MAKING THE MOST
OF FRUIT

—◆◇◆—

We all like to make the most of our chance to eat fresh soft and stone fruits when they come into season. Loaded bushes, trees and vines in the garden or the reappearance of the fruit in the shops, among the year-round citrus, compel our attention, and knowing that their season will be short encourages us to eat our fill. In fact it's easy to serve unadorned fresh summer fruits for dessert at meal after meal and not think beyond them. There may even come a stage when some member of the family says out loud, 'Not strawberries again!'

It does not matter healthwise since we are then — or should be — well supplied with the vitamins and minerals that summer salads and fruits offer. Only you look regretfully at the fruit still on the plants or in the piled shop-windows, and search your memory for alternative ways to serve it — or perhaps think of storing it, if you have the facilities and time.

Storing fruit is like storing sunshine. Bottling, freezing and making whole-fruit conserves are wonderful ways to store summer flavours (and some vitamins) for the grey winter months. If you have a large, dark and airy cellar or attic, suitable varieties of apples and pears can simply be wrapped, each one separately, in newspaper and laid, not touching, on racks or on a dry floor to be kept for winter. Make sure that the fruits are perfect (windfalls will not do).

[156]

Examine them periodically, remove any which show signs of rotting, and check their neighbours for signs of infection. That's really all.

If you do not already do your own bottling, freezing or candying, you will need a specialised textbook. The titles of a few books I have always trusted are on page 196.

You need perfect fruit for all these techniques and for oven-drying. They do not help you use up the less-than-perfect specimens from your few precious back-garden canes or bushes, or on 'special offer' at the greengrocer's or supermarket; still less, overripe fruit which you did not have time to process at its best. Some conserves can help you to use such fruit to advantage. You will find a few jams and similar conserves in Chapter 6 on pages 108–12, for instance; they are fragrant and tasty, but they are very sweet and they lack their original vitamin C, so they are treats not health-helpers.

APPLE AND BLOSSOM.

Fruit juices and syrups are as much work to make as bottled fruits and they lack the fibre which is one of the big assets of whole fruit. Today, too, several natural fruit juices are so widely available in commercial bottles, cans and cartons that it is hardly worth making them, considering the storage space they need. Real *soft* fruit syrups, however, are not easy to get and are quite unlike their commercial counterparts so I've sneakily included one recipe in this chapter which covers them all.

Fruit purées take up much less space than bottled or frozen whole fruit. They are easy to make in these days of food processors and blenders, and although not high on vitamins they use a lot less sugar than jams. You will find a trouble-free way of making these purées in bulk on page 163. Together with whole-fruit pickles and chutneys, they are probably the best way for anyone with limited free time and space to handle imperfect or glut fruit.

Most of the other recipes in this chapter suggest unusual ways of using summer fruits at their peak and also the puréed, stored and dried fruit we rely on later in the year.

[157]

USING FRUIT IN SUMMER

—◆◇—

RHUBARB CAKE *(Makes one 8in/200cm sandwich cake or one 7in/18cm sandwich cake and 12 small buns)*
Rhubarb can pall towards the end of the season when it is coarse and when newer, more attractive seasonal fruits compete with it. Here is an excellent way to make the most of the good nourishment it can still offer. This moist cake will keep well in a tin for a week, if given the chance.

8fl oz/ 200ml puréed stewed
rhubarb (1 cup) (see note)
8oz/200g block margarine,
softened (1 cup)
6–8oz/ 150–200g caster sugar
(³/4–1 cup) depending on purée's
flavour
2 eggs
6oz/150g plain flour (1¹/2 cups)

1¹/4 tsp bicarbonate of soda (1¹/2 tsp
baking soda)
1 scant tsp ground cinnamon (1 tsp)
¹/4 tsp ground cloves (¹/2 tsp)
¹/4 tsp salt (¹/4 tsp)
4fl oz/100ml soured milk (¹/2 cup)
Lemon Curd (page 112)
Lemon Butter Icing (page 76) or
icing sugar (confectioner's sugar)

Grease either two 8in/200mm sandwich tins or one 7in/175mm sandwich tin and twelve 2in/50mm small bun tins (or use paper cases). Taste the rhubarb purée to decide how much sugar to use; if in doubt, use the smaller quantity and add more with the last of the soured milk if needed.

[158]

Cream the margarine and sugar. Beat in the eggs, one at a time. Beat in the rhubarb pulp. Sieve the flour, soda, spices and salt together on to stiff paper. Tip one-third of the dry goods onto the cake batter, beat in briefly, then beat in one-third of the soured milk. Repeat the process twice, using all the ingredients.

Heat the oven to 375°F (190°C), Gas 5. Fill the prepared tins or cases with the cake batter; level the tops of the sandwich layers. Bake the sandwich layers for 20–25 minutes or until springy and beginning to shrink from the sides of the tins. Bake the small cakes at 350°F (180°C), Gas 4 for 20–25 minutes. (In a gas oven, bake these under the sandwich layers, ie on a lower shelf.)

Cool on a wire rack. Then sandwich the cake layers together with lemon curd. Top both large and small cakes with swirls of lemon butter icing, or sprinkle with icing sugar if to be stored or frozen.

Note: For the purée, drain stewed rhubarb over a jug, then purée in a food processor with only just enough of the liquid to make it smooth; elderly rhubarb can be stringy. You will need 1–1¼lb/ 450–600g raw rhubarb, depending on its age and juiciness.

SPARKLING PEACH CONDÉ (Serves 6)
Top-quality home-grown peaches are rare compared with apricots or cherries, and all fresh peaches tend to be expensive to buy. Use the following idea to 'stretch' 2 peaches to serve 6 people.

1 tbsp gelatine (1 tbsp)
one 15½oz/439g can creamed rice
    pudding
2 tbsp caster sugar (2½ tbsp)

2 large fresh peaches
about ½pt/250–275ml sweet
    sparkling Somerset cider (1¼ cups)
3 glacé cherries, halved

Soften the gelatine in 4 tbsp (5 tbsp) cold water, then dissolve it over low heat. Whisk it into the creamed rice with the sugar. Chill until set.

Divide the creamed rice between 6 dessert glasses. Skin the peaches (discard the stones), and cut each into 3 sections. Put 1 section on each rice helping, stoned side down. Immediately before serving, pour cider over each helping and top each peach section with a half cherry.

Note: For a smooth dessert, process the creamed rice in an electric blender, then blend in the dissolved gelatine and sugar.

[159]

FRESH RASPBERRY OR MELBA SAUCE *(Serves 4)*
Probably no lovelier, simpler fruit sauce exists.

8oz/200g fresh raspberries	*3 tbsp white icing sugar, or as needed*
medium-dry white wine, as	*(4 tbsp)*
needed	

Put the hulled raspberries on a plate, and sprinkle them with a little wine and sugar. Leave them for 30 minutes. Then sieve the fruit and any juice and wine with them into a bowl balanced over a pan of hot water. Stir in the rest of the sugar. Add a little more wine if you want a thinner purée. Stir, taste and add a little more sugar if you wish. Cool the purée, and chill before use.

To make a classic Melba dessert, poach 4 skinned fresh peaches or pears with a vanilla pod and sugar. Drain and cool, then lay them in a bowl lined with ½pt/250ml (1¼ cups) vanilla ice cream. Pour ⅛pt/ 65ml (good ¼ cup) raspberry sauce over them, and sprinkle toasted flaked almonds on top.

Variations:
Use strawberries or loganberries instead of raspberries.

RASPBERRY POT PIE *(serves 4)*
Colour picture page 117

1lb/450g hulled raspberries	*2½oz/65g caster sugar (¼ cup +*
2½oz/65g butter (¼ cup +	*1 tbsp)*
1 tbsp)	*1 tsp ground ginger (1 tsp)*
4oz/100g sifted plain flour	*a few raspberries to decorate*
(1 cup)	*whipped cream*

Put the raspberries into a 1¼pt/600ml (3 cup) soufflé dish or similar deep baking dish. Rub the butter into the flour, and mix in the sugar and ginger. Pile the crumble mixture on the fruit. Bake at 350°F (180°C), Gas 4 for 50 minutes. Cool. Decorate with a few whole raspberries and serve with whipped cream.

Variations:
You can use other fresh soft or stone fruit, such as hulled loganberries or strawberries, stoned halved apricots or plums.

FRESH SOFT FRUIT SYRUPS

Fruit syrups make refreshing drinks with water or soda water. You can use them for making milk shakes too, and fresh fruit jellies. Add a few spoonfuls to a fruit salad, a trifle or other desserts, or pour a little over vanilla ice cream as a topping.

Use any of the following fruits: blackberries, blackcurrants, gooseberries, loganberries, raspberries, redcurrants, strawberries. Any ripe or near-ripe fruit which is not mildewed or mouldy is suitable. Pick over the fruit and remove any which is decayed.

You will also need ¾lb/350g (scant 1½ cups) sugar to each 1pt/ 500ml (2½ cups) juice.

GOOSEBERRY.

Add ½pt/250ml (1¼ cups) water to each 1lb/450g blackcurrants or to each 6lb/2.5kg blackberries — other fruits do not need water. Heat the fruit in a basin over a pan of boiling water, or very gently in a preserving pan, until the juice begins to run freely. Crush the fruit with a wooden spoon, and strain through a jelly bag or press out the juice in a cloth. Measure the juice and put it into a saucepan or preserving pan. Add ¾lb/350g (scant 1½ cups) sugar to each 1pt/ 500ml (2½ cups) juice. Place over very gentle heat just until the sugar is fully dissolved. Pour the syrup into clean screw-topped preserving jars, leaving a good ½in/10mm headspace. Screw on the tops, then unscrew to loosen slightly.

Stand the bottles on thick newspaper in a deep pan of cold water which must come to within 1in/2.5cm of the tops of the bottles. Heat the water to simmering point, and hold it for 20 minutes. Remove the bottles on to sheets of stout paper or a wooden work top, and tighten the screw tops. After 10 minutes, tighten the tops again. Cool well, label, and store.

Note: Once opened, use all the syrup within 2 days if you keep it in a larder, or within 10 days if kept in a refrigerator.

[161]

SOMERSET PLUM SYLLABUB *(Serves 4–6)*

Plums are late summer fruit. Knowing that autumn was near, cooks in the past always made an effort to use or preserve the crop, even in glut years.

1/2pt/250ml plum purée made like Apple Purée, page 163 (1 1/4 cups)
4fl oz/100ml double cream (1/2 cup heavy cream)
6fl oz/150ml (1 small can) evaporated milk (3/4 cup)

4oz/100g caster sugar (1/2 cup)
2 1/2fl oz/65ml sweet Somerset cider (1/4 cup + 1 tbsp)
2 tbsp lemon juice or to taste (2 1/2 tbsp)
2 egg whites, whisked until stiff
candied angelica, to decorate

Cool the purée if freshly made. Whip the double (heavy) cream until stiff, adding the evaporated milk slowly while whisking. Fold in the plum purée, then add the other ingredients in order, folding in the whisked egg whites last. Spoon into individual dessert glasses.

Chill for 2 hours. Scatter a few shreds of candied angelica on top of each syllabub before serving.

EVESHAM CRUMBLE *(Serves 4)*

Greengages are the last of the season's home-grown stone fruit, so make the most of them. This baked dessert is just right for the first chilly days in September.

3oz/75g medium oatmeal (1/2 cup)
ground cinnamon to taste
2oz/50g 85 per cent extraction flour (1/2 cup)
3oz/75g slightly salted butter (1/3 cup)

2oz/50g muscovado or golden granulated sugar (1/4 cup)
1lb/450g greengages, halved and stoned
granulated sugar, to taste

Mix the oatmeal and cinnamon, and sift in the flour. Return any bran in the sifter to the dry mixture. Rub in the butter until the mixture is crumbly. Mix in the sugar.

Put the greengages into a shallow ovenproof serving dish. Sprinkle with granulated sugar. Cover with the crumble. Bake at 375°F (190°C), Gas 5 for 40–45 minutes until the fruit is cooked and the topping is crunchy. Serve hot.

QUICK APPLE PURÉE OR SAUCE *(Makes about 1pt/500ml [2½ cups])*

It is hardly worth while making a small quantity of apple purée by the oven method (below), so if you want enough just for one or two dishes, use this recipe.

2lb/1kg cooking apples	*1 tbsp butter or margarine*
5 tbsp water (6 tbsp)	*(1¼ tbsp)*
squeeze of lemon juice	*clear honey to taste (for sweetened*
2 cloves or 1in/2.5cm piece	*purée or sauce)*
cinnamon stick	

Quarter and core the apples; chop roughly, cutting out any worm-holes. Put in a saucepan with the water, lemon juice, flavouring and fat. Cover tightly, and simmer for about 20 minutes or until apples are very soft.

Mash with a wooden spoon, then sieve. Stir in any honey you want, then reheat if necessary before using.

APPLE PURÉE

A purée of apples is just familiar apple sauce, but for savoury dishes and cakes it should be less sweet. It is a fine standby to freeze in bulk, unsweetened, since it can be used in a dozen different ways.

To make it the trouble-free way, chop the apples roughly, including peel and cores. You can mix cooking and eating apples, and use up windfalls, misshapen, or shrivelled stored apples provided they are not decayed, wormy or badly bruised. Sprinkle the fruit well with lemon juice, and spice it by adding 2 cloves or a 1in/2.5cm piece of cinnamon stick to each 1lb/450g fruit. Pack it in a heavy oven-proof pot with not more than 3in/7.5cm depth of water in the bottom; use just enough water to prevent the apples drying out before their own juices run. Seal the pot securely. Bake at the lowest possible heat for several hours or overnight.

Cool the purée slightly, then sieve it with a little extra lemon juice to prevent discolouring. Turn it into a rigid plastic container, cool, seal and freeze it. Frozen purée should keep well for 3–4 months. Otherwise bottle it, sweetened, in the same way as whole fruit. Use small bottles because you probably will not need much purée at a time, eg for apple sauce. Leave frozen purée unsweetened until you need it, then sweeten to suit your dish.

You can purée pears or firm stone fruits in the same way, with or without the spices as you prefer.

[163]

FARMHOUSE BRAN APPLECAKE *(Serves 3–4)*

A good 'hidden' way to add extra fibre to family meals is to use a bran-type breakfast cereal in desserts.

*1/2pt/250ml thick unsweetened
  apple purée (1 1/4 cups)
  (page 163)*
*2oz/50g fresh white breadcrumbs
  (1 cup)*
grated rind of 1/2 lemon
caster sugar as needed

*6oz Toasted Farmhouse Bran
  (about 3 cups)*
3oz/75g butter (1/3 cup)
*1 tbsp golden granulated sugar
  (1 1/4 tbsp)*
oil for greasing
blackcurrant jam, to decorate

Use a pale-green apple purée to contrast with the dark bran. Mix in the white breadcrumbs to make it really thick, the lemon rind and enough caster sugar to sweeten well.

Process the Toasted Farmhouse Bran to coarse crumbs in a food processor or blender, or with a rolling pin. Melt the butter, add the bran crumbs, and toss over low heat until well coated. Remove from the heat, and mix in the golden granulated sugar. Cool slightly.

Oil a 1¼pt/625ml soufflé dish or charlotte mould. Press an even layer of crumbs over the bottom. Cover with a layer of purée. Repeat the layers until all the ingredients are used, ending with crumbs.

Chill under a light weight for 24 hours. Turn out, and decorate with small blobs of blackcurrant jam. Use as a dessert.

USING FRUIT IN AUTUMN AND WINTER

——◆◇◆——

BACON AND APPLE PIE *(Serves 8)*
In the old days, any farm would have made its own cheese, cured its own bacon, and used its own orchard apples. However, even today, this dish makes a cheap, substantial family meal.

PASTRY:
12oz/300g plain flour (3 cups)
3oz/75g butter (¹/₃ cup)
3oz/75g lard (¹/₃ cup)
1 egg, beaten
2 tbsp milk or as needed (2¹/₂ tbsp)

FILLING:
3 large cooking apples (can be
  windfalls)
salt, pepper and grated nutmeg,
  to taste
9oz/225g mature cheese, shredded
  (2¹/₄ cups)
6oz/150g piece boiling bacon without
  rind, chopped
7oz/175g mashed potato (scant 1 cup)
1 tbsp melted butter (1¹/₄ tbsp)

BOTTLE-JACK AND WHEEL,
WITH JOINT SUSPENDED.

Line and grease a 7¹/₂in/185mm loose-bottomed cake tin, 3in/75mm deep. Sift the flour, and rub in the fats. Beat the egg into the milk, and use to bind the mixture; it should leave the sides of the bowl clean. Press the pastry evenly all over the base and sides of the tin.

Peel and core the apples, slice into thin rounds, and cut the slices in half. Cover the pastry base with a third of the apple slices, and season lightly with salt, pepper and nutmeg. Sprinkle with a third of the cheese, and cover with a third of the bacon. Repeat the layers twice. Spread the mashed potato on top, score with a fork, and brush with melted butter.

Bake at 325°F (160°C), Gas 3 for 1¹/₄–1¹/₂ hours. Serve hot with a paper frill round the tin; or cool in the tin, unmould and serve cold.

[165]

MARROW WITH HOT SALAD STUFFING *(Serves 4–6)*
Stretch meat by adding tangy fruit, aromatic herbs and crunchy seeds as an exciting filling for a normally unexciting vegetable.

1 large marrow
2 tbsp margarine (2¹/₂ tbsp)
8oz/200g beef mince (2 cups)
1 medium-sized onion, chopped
1 small cooking apple, peeled and
* chopped*
4oz/100g lettuce, finely shredded
1 small tomato, chopped

1¹/₂ tbsp hulled sunflower seeds
* (2 tbsp)*
¹/₂ tsp cider vinegar (³/₄ tsp)
salt and pepper
¹/₄ tsp dried thyme (¹/₂ tsp)
¹/₂ tsp crushed dried basil (³/₄ tsp)
buttered brown breadcrumbs,
* for topping*

Cut the marrow in half lengthways, scrape out the seeds and fibre, and spread the cut sides with half the margarine. Place cut-side down in a baking tin, and bake at 400°F (200°C), Gas 6 for 20–25 minutes.

Meanwhile, sauté the mince in the remaining margarine until lightly browned. Add the onion, apple, lettuce, tomato and seeds. Simmer, turning over as required, until tender. Add the vinegar, seasoning and herbs and mix well.

Turn the marrow halves cut-side up, and fill with the mince mixture. Sprinkle with buttered crumbs and bake for another 20 minutes.

Variation:
Use the same mixture and method for stuffing aubergines.

CHEESE POTS *(Serves 4 as a starter)*
An interesting way to make the most of a couple of windfalls or slightly bruised fruits. Lancashire cheese, especially Farmhouse English Lancashire, is famous as a toasting cheese and traditional in north-country apple pies.
Colour picture page 34.

1 apple
1 pear
1 stalk celery
2 tsp lemon juice (2¹/₂ tsp)

1–2 tsp chopped chives (1¹/₄ tsp)
8oz/200g Lancashire cheese (2 cups)
paprika
2 tsp chopped parsley (2¹/₂ tsp)

Core and dice the apple and pear. Chop the celery. Toss them together in the lemon juice, and add the chives. Divide the mixture between 4 ramekin dishes, Crumble the cheese over each dish.

Put under a medium-hot grill for 5–10 minutes until golden

brown. Sprinkle with paprika and chopped parsley just before serving.

Offer fingers of hot toasted Herb Bread (page 84) with these savoury pots.

APPLE PUDDING *(Serves 8)*

BUTTERCRUST PASTRY:
6oz/150g self-raising flour
  (1½ cups)
4½oz/110g wholemeal self-
  raising flour (rounded 1 cup)
1½oz/35g fresh wholemeal
  breadcrumbs (rounded ¾ cup)
½ tsp salt (¾ tsp)
5oz/125g unsalted butter, flaked
  (½ cup + 2 tbsp)
cold water to mix

FILLING:
1½lb/700g cooking apples
grated rind of 1 lemon
6oz/150g seedless raisins (1 cup)
3oz/75g golden granulated sugar
  (⅓ cup) or to taste
¼ tsp grated nutmeg (¼ tsp)

SAUCE:
juice of 1 lemon or to taste
½pt/250ml sweetened cold custard
  (1¼ cups)

Grease a 2¼pt/1.2 litre pudding basin. Mix together both flours, the breadcrumbs and salt. Rub in the fat. Mix to a firm dough with cold water. Chill, then roll out just over half the pastry into a circle ¾in/2cm larger than the diameter of the basin. Lift the pastry into the basin, and shape it to form a lining, pressing out folds and bringing the pastry up to the top of the basin. From the remaining pastry, cut out 3 circles to fit the basin at 3 levels; one should fit the top of the basin.

Peel, quarter, core and slice the apples. Mix them with the lemon rind, raisins, sugar and nutmeg.

Put a layer of mixed fruit in the basin, and completely cover with a layer of pastry. Repeat the layers twice, sealing the top layer of pastry to the edge of the lining pastry, by pinching them together. Cover the pudding securely with greased foil.

Stand the basin on a cloth or thick newspaper in a heavy saucepan, and pour in enough boiling water to come half-way up its sides. Cover the saucepan, and steam the pudding for 1½–2 hours. Leave to stand in the basin, uncovered, for 10 minutes. Serve from the basin, or turned out onto a warmed plate.

For the sauce, mix the lemon juice into the sweetened cold custard.

PEAR AND COCONUT CRUMBLE *(Serves 6)*

This simple dessert is good hot or cold. Coconut provides its fibre content.

6oz/150g apricot jam (about ½ cup)
2fl oz/50ml medium dry white wine or cider (¼ cup)
1 tbsp water (1¼ tbsp)

2oz/50g butter or margarine (¼ cup)
1½lb/700g firm eating pears
2 tbsp desiccated coconut (2½ tbsp)
5 bought coconut macaroons
extra apricot jam for serving

Sieve the jam and mix it with the wine or cider and water. Grease an oven-to-table baking dish 8in/200mm across and 1½in/35mm deep with 1 tbsp (1¼ tbsp) of the fat. Peel, quarter and core the pears, and cut them into thick slices lengthways. Sprinkle them with the coconut, then lay them in neat overlapping circles in the dish. Pour the jam and wine over them at once.

Crumble the macaroons, discarding any rice paper, and scatter them all over the pears. Flake the remaining fat over the macaroon crumbs and bake at 375°F (190°C), Gas 5 for 20 minutes or until the macaroon crumbs are golden. Serve hot or cold with warmed apricot jam.

Note: You could use home-made fresh apricot purée instead of jam.

[168]

APPLE PURÉE WITH CHUTNEY *(Serves 5–6)*
A windfall purée, using late fallen or stored fruit, which makes a fine, cheap, spicy accompaniment to autumn game, duck or a braised bacon joint. It adds a fillip to grilled or barbecued sausages too.

about 4lb/1.8kg cooking apples
grated nutmeg
2 tbsp softened butter (2¹/₂ tbsp)

2–4 tbsp apricot or mango chutney
(2¹/₂–5 tbsp)
salt and pepper

Peel, core, and slice or chop the apples. Simmer them in a saucepan with very little water and a pinch of nutmeg, over low heat, until soft; turn them over often while cooking, to prevent scorching. Stir in the butter, and continue cooking until all the water has been driven off, stirring often. Sieve the apple for a smooth-based purée.

Chop any large bits of fruit in the chutney finely, then mix the chutney into the apple purée. Season to taste. Reheat, or serve cold, depending on the dish you want to eat it with.

Citrus and dried fruit

FIG FILLER *(Makes about 1¹/₄lb/600g filling or spread)*
Figs are the least popular of the dried fruit, yet can be surprisingly useful. You will find some ideas for using this simple 'filler' or spread at the end of the recipe.

1lb/450g dried figs
2 egg yolks, well beaten
1 tbsp lemon juice or to taste
(1¹/₄ tbsp)

finely chopped parsley to taste
salt and pepper

Pour boiling water over the figs and soak for several hours until soft. Drain. Chop finely; then sieve, or purée in a food processor or electric blender. Put the purée in a saucepan and stir over low heat until it is steaming. Off the heat, stir in the egg yolks quickly. Leave for 5 minutes, then mix in the lemon juice, parsley and seasoning.

Turn the mixture into small jars, cover loosely with circles of waxed paper, and cool. Cover, and refrigerate until wanted. Use within 4 weeks.

Here are some ways to use the filler:
Spread it on slices of ham, roll up the slices like baby Swiss rolls, and serve them with salad.

Stuff the belly cavity of a mackerel with filler before grilling it; serve a little fig filler with the fish instead of gooseberry sauce.

Use the filler to stuff the core holes of apples before baking them as a garnish for roast pork, bacon or ham.

Use the filler as a sandwich spread; or spread it on buttered toast, cover it with thin slivers of cheese and grill it.

ST GEORGE'S PIE *(Serves 6)*

Crusaders brought us our patron saint, encouraged by finding him worshipped in Spain. Naturally, therefore, the feast dish most associated with him is a medieval-style pot pie rich with the dried fruit and spices which the Crusaders also brought home.

FOR THE PASTRY:
7oz/175g white flour (1³/4 cups)
1oz/25g wholemeal flour (¹/4 cup)
2oz/50g butter (¹/4 cup)
2oz/50g lard (¹/4 cup)
water to mix

FOR THE FILLING:
1¹/2lb/700g boneless lamb
2 medium onions
1lb/450g sharp apples

8 prunes
12 dried apricots
1 tsp grated orange rind (1¹/4 tsp)
¹/2 tsp grated nutmeg
¹/2 tsp each ground cinnamon,
*   mace and allspice (¹/2 tsp)*
salt and ground black pepper
clear honey, if needed
¹/4pt/125ml lamb gravy or stock
*   (¹/2 cup + 2 tbsp)*

Make the pastry in the usual way. Chill while preparing the filling.

Slice the meat into small pieces. Skin and slice the onions. Peel and core the apples and slice thinly. Stone and chop the prunes, and chop the apricots. Arrange the meat and fruits in layers in a greased 2¼–2½pt/1.2–1.4 litre earthenware casserole, sprinkling each layer with grated orange rind, spices and seasoning. If the apples are very sharp, sprinkle with a little clear honey. When all the ingredients are used — and they should fill the casserole well — trickle in the gravy or stock.

Roll out the pastry (¼in/5mm thick) and lay it on the top of the casserole. Seal to the rim. Decorate with trimmings. Cut small slits for steam to escape. Bake at 400°F (200°C), Gas 6 for 20 minutes. Reduce the heat to 325°F (160°C), Gas 3 and bake for another 45–50 minutes. Serve hot with apricot chutney.

FARMHOUSE PLUM PUDDING *(Makes two 2lb/900g puddings)*

It's hardly worth while assembling these ingredients and using the fuel just to make one pudding. Make two, and use one as a Christmas Pudding. Use within 6 weeks.

1lb/450g wholemeal breadcrumbs (8 cups)	8oz/200g seedless raisins (1⅓ cups)
¼ tsp each ground mace, cinnamon and ginger (¼ tsp each)	2oz/50g currants (⅓ cup)
	4oz/100g chopped mixed peel (⅔ cup)
¼ tsp grated nutmeg (½ tsp)	4oz/100g grated carrot or apple (⅔ cup)
1 tsp salt (1¼ tsp)	
8oz/200g golden granulated sugar (1 cup)	2 tbsp brandy (2½ tbsp)
	3 tbsp milk (4 tbsp)
8oz/200g shredded suet, home-made or bought (1 cup)	2 tbsp natural apple juice (2½ tbsp)
	2 eggs
10oz/250g sultanas (1⅔ cups)	2 tbsp warmed honey (2½ tbsp)

Mix together the breadcrumbs, spices, salt and sugar. Stir in the suet, dried fruit, peel and carrot or apple. Mix the brandy, milk and juice, and beat in the eggs. Use to bind the dry ingredients.

Grease two 2pt/1.1 litre pudding basins and circles of greaseproof paper to cover the puddings. Half fill a large stewpan or fish kettle with water, and lay a thick cloth in the bottom. Then spoon the pudding mixture into the basins, and cover securely with the greaseproof paper and with foil, leaving room for the puddings to expand.

Put the basins in the pan, cover and bring to the boil; cook gently for 6–8 hours, topping up the water when needed. Cool. Cover with clean dry foil but do not remove the paper. Store in a cool dry place. Boil again for 2 hours before use.

[171]

MINCEMEAT *(Makes about 2½lb/1.1kg)*
A good standby all through the winter, not just at Christmas time.
Use a little for stuffing the core holes in apples before baking, as a
filling for pancakes or a boned lamb joint.

8oz/200g currants (1⅓ cups)
8oz/200g sultanas
(1⅓ cups golden raisins)
8oz/200g raisins (1⅓ cups)
8oz/200g grated apple (1⅓ cups)
4oz/100g chopped mixed peel
(⅔ cup)
2oz/50g flaked almonds
(scant ½ cup)

4oz/100g soft brown sugar (½ cup)
½ tsp ground ginger (¾ tsp)
½ tsp grated nutmeg (¾ tsp)
1 tsp mixed spice (1¼ tsp)
grated rind and juice of 1 lemon
4oz/100g margarine, melted (½ cup)
4 tbsp brandy or whisky, optional
(5 tbsp)

Mix all the ingredients thoroughly in a bowl. Pack into sterile dry
jars. Seal securely and store in a cool dry place.

BOTTLED ORANGES
Syrupy bottled oranges make a winter treat and can make good use
of a 'special offer'. They are bottled in much the same way as other
fruit. Here is the time-honoured 'cold-water bath' method.

2oz/50g sugar (¼ cup)
1pt/500ml water (2½ cups)

8–12 oranges

Make a sugar syrup first by putting the sugar and water in a pan over
moderate heat, and stirring until the sugar dissolves. Cool.

Dip the oranges in boiling water; then remove the peel, all pith
and any visible pips but leave the fruit whole. Pack the fruit into a
3½pt/1.5 litre preserving jar which has been boiled. Pour in the
syrup, tapping the jar to get rid of air bubbles; fill to within ¼in/
5mm of the top of the jar.

If the jar has a screw-band, put on the rubber ring, glass top and
band, then unscrew enough to loosen the band slightly. Put the jar
in a large deep pan, with thick newspaper in the bottom. Fill the pan
with cold water up to the neck of the bottle and, very slowly, bring
the water to 175°F/165°C (take 1½ hours to do it). Keep it at this
temperature for 15 minutes.

Remove the jar from the water, and tighten the screw-band if
used. Tighten it again after 3–4 hours. Next day, hold the jar upside
down over a basin, to test that it has sealed. Label. Store in a cool dry
place and use as a dessert within 6 months.

PRUNE SPICE CAKE (Makes one 8in/20cm ring, or sandwich, cake)

1lb/450g prunes
6oz/150g muscovado sugar
  (3/4 cup)
8oz/200g margarine (1 cup)
2 eggs
6oz/150g 85 per cent extraction
  flour (1 1/2 cups)
1 1/2 tsp bicarbonate of soda (2 tsp)

1 tsp ground cinnamon (1 1/4 tsp)
1/2 tsp ground cloves (3/4 tsp)
1/4 tsp ground allspice (1/4 tsp)
1/2 tsp salt (1/2 tsp)
4fl oz/100ml slightly sour milk
  (1/2 cup)
2oz/50g flaked almonds, crushed
  (1/2 cup)

Put the prunes in a saucepan and pour over just enough boiling water to cover them. Leave to stand for 3–4 hours. Then simmer in the same water for about 20 minutes until very soft. Add a little more water if needed, but as little as possible. Drain the prunes and let them cool. When cool, stone and pound the skins and flesh to a pulp, or purée them in a food processor or electric blender.

Grease an 8in/200mm ring cake tin, or use an ordinary cake tin with a 1lb/450g jam jar in the centre. For a sandwich cake grease two 8in/200mm sandwich tins.

Beat the sugar and margarine together until soft and creamy. Beat in the eggs, one at a time, then the prune pulp. Mix the flour, soda, spices and salt in a second bowl. Add the dry mixture to the prune mixture in three parts, alternately with the sour milk. Beat well after each addition. Lastly, stir in the flaked almonds. Turn the cake mixture into the prepared ring cake tin, without shifting the jar if you use it. Alternatively spoon the mixture into the two sandwich tins.

Bake the ring cake at 350°F (180°C), Gas 4 for 30 minutes, then raise the heat to 375°F (190°C), Gas 5 and bake for another 30 minutes or until the cake loosens slightly from the sides of the tin. Cool in the tin for 15 minutes, then turn onto a wire rack to finish cooling. Wrap and store in an airtight tin.

Bake the two sandwich cake layers at 375°F (190°C), Gas 5 for about 30 minutes. Cool on a wire rack. Sandwich together with a thin layer of plum jam.

Variation:
Cover either cake with lemon glacé icing, and decorate with a ring of seeded raisins.

MRS BEETON'S SCHOOL CAKE *(Makes 1 7in/18cm square cake)*

Mrs Beeton actually called this 'a common cake to send to children at school'. Originally, it was probably a piece of the weekly bread dough, enriched with seeds, spice and dried fruit for a Sunday treat.

1½ tbsp dried yeast (1½ tbsp)
½pt/250ml tepid milk (1¼ cups)
good pinch of sugar
1lb/450g plain flour (4 cups)
2oz/50g clarified dripping, not too
 hard (¼ cup)
good pinch of salt (depending on
 flavour of dripping)
2 tbsp caraway seeds, optional
 (2½ tbsp)
1 tsp ground allspice (1 tsp)
4oz/100g light soft brown sugar
 (½ cup)
8oz/200g currants (1⅓ cups)

CURRANTS.

Sprinkle the yeast on the milk with the pinch of sugar. Leave until frothy. Put the flour in a bowl, and rub in the fat. Mix in all the other dry ingredients. Make a well in the centre and pour in the yeast liquid. Mix well, then knead thoroughly with floured hands.

Line and grease a square 7in/175mm tin. Turn in the mixture and level the top. Leave in a warm place for 1–1½ hours until well risen. Bake at 425°F (220°C), Gas 7 for 15–20 minutes, then lower the heat to 350°F (180°C), Gas 4 and bake for another 30 minutes or until the cake tests done when a heated skewer put into the centre comes out clean. Cool on a rack.

Variation:
Use only 6oz/150g (1 cup) currants and 1 tsp (1¼ tsp) lemon rind — my idea, not Mrs Beeton's.

10

EXTRA FLAVOUR TO YOUR FOOD

—◆◇◆—

Curing food just means preserving it, usually with salt, sometimes helped by smoke. If salt really penetrates any food, it prevents bacteria growing more effectively than any other method except making the food bone-dry. So pickling, which means curing foods which are still moist, means in effect preserving in salt. The salted food can be dried as it is, or it can be smoked. The resins in the smoke help to preserve the food too.

Salting and smoking have been home crafts for centuries, although we have almost forgotten them since Victorian times. As families became smaller, cooks no longer needed to keep whole sides of bacon or two or three whole hams ready for use, and stopped curing their own meat. Fish has always been pickled commercially. As for vegetables, cooks stopped salting their beans in barrels, drying their mushrooms and so on when it became easier to buy them in cans or, later, frozen. So the old crafts slipped into disuse.

This is a pity in a way because doing one's own curing can be both economical and interesting. One can pickle cheap cuts of meat bought in bulk or on special offer, or make good use of an angler's catch, thus saving freezer space and gaining more intriguing products than one can buy.

However, home pickling and smoking demand both space and

[175]

time, probably more than most busy people are prepared to give, and they do take practice. So if you are lucky enough to have access to bulk pork products, game meat or a whole salmon which you need to preserve without freezing, your easiest step will be to take it to a local bacon factory, and make use of its craftsmen's expertise. For the rest of us, the sensible course is to make the best use we can of the many preserved, salted and smoked products available.

In this section, therefore, you will find recipes which make the best use of some of our more economical preserved meats — the cheaper cuts of bacon for instance, and British sausages.

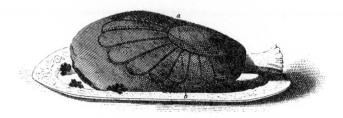

H A M

Bacon, ham and sausages
Bacon and ham are two of our oldest and most versatile cured meats. Once the peasant's standby, a small bacon or gammon joint is now, however, not cheap. It is wise therefore to take some trouble to make the best use of it, to cook it well, and to make it do double duty as a meat and a flavouring agent — for instance by using the rinds to flavour a stew in the time-honoured way, or by mixing leftover scraps with poultry or other mild meats.

One can also economise by buying and using cheaper meats than prime back bacon and fine York ham. Pickled pork boiled and served with pease pudding is a first-class traditional dish in its own right. It can also be substituted for ham in a number of other dishes, such as veal and ham pie, without any real loss, or it can 'double' as gammon or bacon rashers.

Many people have favourite recipe books which call for a slice or two of ham among other ingredients. In this case, it is commonsense to step sideways from the 'natural foods' and use one of the cheaper vacuum-packed ham products. But choose a pure meat product rather than one with preserved vegetable or stuffing added — any additions to the contents are stated on the pack label.

Sausages, whether cured and smoked or made of fresh raw meat, are one of the oldest processed foods, and one of the most varied and

[176]

interesting to use. The Romans counted them among their favourite meats, and made dozens of different types. Some were festival foods. One Roman emperor tried to ban sausages from the empire because they became closely associated with the feast of Lupercalia, notorious for licentious orgies. He failed completely.

The Roman armies marched with smoked sausages in their knapsacks, and wherever they went this new food proved a lasting success. Even today, the Germans and Italians in particular make types of sausage almost unchanged since Roman times, besides many others. Any good delicatessen carries a wide variety of these continental sausages: heavily smoked, dried ones; lightly smoked or cooked ones for eating as they are, or for boiling; fresh ones such as liver sausage which can be almost as soft as clotted cream. Some are bland, others strongly aromatic or garlicky. They are all fairly expensive, but even a tiny piece of one of the full-flavoured sausages will make a stew or casserole aromatic, so an inch or two is worth buying sometimes for foreign dishes.

Cost isn't a factor in British 'bangers'. Curiously, although Europeans took so avidly to smoked sausages, we didn't. Ours are among the few fresh raw sausages made for cooking, and they are unusual in other ways. Almost all of them are made predominantly just of one meat, usually pork or beef. Unlike continental ones, our pork sausages can contain up to 35 per cent cereal and beef ones up to 50 per cent. Unlike most continental ones too, their fat and lean are minced together to make a crumbly mix which is the same all the way through; and of course their spicing and flavour are unique.

You can make various kinds of sausages at home, but they can be filled evenly only if you possess a sausage-filling funnel or mechanical appliance, or an attachment to an electric mixer. Hand-filling is not satisfactory unless you are experienced at it. You must be prepared, too, to buy the large number of sausage casings sold in a single pack, unless you can persuade a friendly butcher to sell you a few from his stock. By and large, the investment and trouble are not really worth while just to make one, distinctively flavoured, product. Either make one of the many traditional types of skinless sausage or use your butcher's, or commercially-made ones. Bought British 'bangers' are always available in several forms and sizes, and they can be one of your best standbys for cheap, quick yet nourishing meals.

You needn't just fry or grill them; there are lots of different ways to use them, as the recipes included in this chapter show.

[177]

SALTED AND SMOKED MEATS

—◆◇—

CHOUCROUTE GARNIE *(Serves 8)*

8oz/200g piece of streaky bacon weighed with rind removed (see method)
large pieces of bacon rind, about 8oz/200g
2 carrots
2¹/₂lb/1.1kg canned sauerkraut
8oz/200g boiling sausage (not black pudding) in one piece
1lb/450g pork spare ribs
8 small Frankfurter sausages (chipolata size)

2 onions, skinned, each stuck with a clove
bouquet garni including 12 juniper berries
3oz/75g chicken fat or lard (¹/₃ cup)
about ³/₄pt/375ml Alsatian white wine (2 cups)
4fl oz/100ml vegetable stock (¹/₂ cup)
fat for greasing

You can use any rind on your piece of bacon to make up the weight of pieces you will need; it may be the most convenient way to get it. Only remember that you must buy a heavier piece of meat than 8oz/ 200g in weight to allow for it.

Slice the bacon, and blanch the slices in boiling water for 3 minutes. Line the bottom and sides of a large flameproof casserole with pieces of bacon rind. Slice the carrots thinly. Drain the sauer-kraut, and put about half of it into the casserole in an even layer, mixed with the carrot. Cover with the blanched bacon slices. Lay the piece of boiling sausage, the spare ribs and the Frankfurter saus-ages on the bacon. Cover with the rest of the sauerkraut. Lay the onions on top. Tuck the bouquet garni among the vegetables. Add the fat in small dabs, and the wine and stock. Do not add any salt and pepper.

Cover the casserole tightly with greased foil, then with a lid, and simmer or bake at 325°F (160°C), Gas 3 for 2½ hours. Remove and discard the onions and the bouquet garni. Take out the meats and bacon and slice neatly the boiling sausage and spare ribs.

Pile the sauerkraut on a large warmed dish and arrange the sliced meats, bacon and whole Frankfurters in a decorative pattern on top. Serve with boiled potatoes sprinkled with caraway or dill seeds.

SLIPPER PUDDING (Serves 4)
Gammon slipper is a small smoked pork joint from the lower end of the gammon hock or thigh of a pig. It costs slightly more than the forehock slipper (from the foreleg), but it is leaner and bigger, weighing about 1½lb/700g.

1½lb/700g gammon slipper
4oz/100g small Sofa Mushrooms
    (page 137) (1½ cups)
1oz/25g flour (¼ cup)
freshly ground black pepper
juice of ½ lemon

PASTRY:
8oz/200g plain flour (2 cups)
2 tsp baking powder (2½ tsp)
½ tsp salt (¾ tsp)
4oz/100g shredded suet (beef fat)
    (½ cup)
¼pt/125ml water (½ cup + 2 tbsp)

Put the meat into cold water, bring to the boil and drain. Cut into ½in/1cm cubes. Quarter the mushrooms; keep aside, separately.

To make the pastry, mix the flour, baking powder, salt and suet. Add the water gradually, mixing in with a knife to make a soft dough. Grease a 1½pt/850ml (2pt) pudding basin and line it with two-thirds of the pastry, keeping the rest for the top.

Toss the meat with the 1oz/25g flour. Fill the basin with alternate layers of meat and mushrooms, seasoning each layer with a little pepper. When full, pour the lemon juice over the filling. Cover the pudding with the remaining pastry, sealing it to the edge of the basin. Cover securely with greased foil, leaving room for the pud-ding to rise slightly.

Stand the pudding on a trivet or cloth in a pan of boiling water which comes half-way up its sides. Cover and cook for about 3 hours, topping up the water if needed.

Remove the foil, and stand the basin in a decorative bowl for bringing to the table. Serve with buttered broad beans or celeriac simmered in butter.

HONEY-GLAZED COLLAR OF BACON *(Serves 5–6)*

Cheap as joints go, and useful if visitors come for Sunday lunch. An excellent buy for two people as well, since when cold it can be sliced and used like ham.

2lb/900g bacon collar (neck cut salt pork)
4 whole cloves

2 bay leaves
1 tbsp clear honey (1 1/4 tbsp)

Put meat in a large pan and cover with cold water. Bring to the boil slowly. Drain. Cover with fresh water. Add the cloves and bay leaves. Bring to the boil, lower the heat and simmer, half-covered, for 20 minutes per 1lb/25 minutes per 500g.

Remove from the pan to a board, using two large forks. Cool slightly, then pare or strip the skin off evenly. Score the fat into diamond shapes, and brush with the honey. Put in the oven at 400°F (200°C), Gas 6 for 10 minutes. Serve with short-cooked vegetables in season.

SAUSAGE AND APPLE DUMPLINGS *(Serves 8)*

These are easy to serve for brunch, Sunday supper or an informal teenage party.

Colour picture page 118

SUET PASTRY:
10oz/250g plain flour (2 1/2 cups)
1 1/2 tsp baking powder (2 tsp)
5oz/125g shredded suet (beef fat)
(1/2 cup + 2 tbsp)
pinch of salt and ground black pepper

cold water to mix
beaten egg

1lb/450g pork sausage meat
1 cooking apple
2 tbsp Sweet Carrot and Apple Pickle (2 1/2 tbsp) (page 189)

Make the pastry first by mixing the flour, baking powder, suet and seasoning. Make a well in the centre, and add enough water to make a soft pliable dough. Divide into 8 equal portions and roll each out into a 7in/175mm circle.

[180]

Divide the sausage meat into 8 equal-sized flat rounds. Peel and core the apple and cut it into 8 chunks. Place an apple chunk and a little pickle on each sausage-meat round, and fold the sausage meat round, to cover. Place each sausage-meat portion in the centre of a pastry round, and close the pastry round it.

Place the dumplings on a greased baking sheet, and brush the tops with beaten egg. Bake at 375°F (190°C), Gas 5 for 25–30 minutes, or until the pastry is cooked through and golden. Serve hot with baked tomatoes, or use as a cold packed meal.

SAUSAGE, LEEK AND CIDER BAKE *(Serves 4)*
Few dishes could be more British than 'bangers' teamed with cider, English mustard and Farmhouse Cheddar.
Colour picture page 135

4 leeks, washed and trimmed
1lb/450g fresh pork sausages
1oz/25g butter (2 tbsp)
1oz/25g flour (¹/4 cup)
¹/4pt/125ml milk (¹/2 cup + 2 tbsp)
¹/4pt/125ml dry still cider (¹/2 cup + 2 tbsp)
¹/2 tsp made English mustard or to taste (³/4 tsp)
2oz/50g grated Cheddar cheese (Farmhouse English cheese if possible) (¹/2 cup)
salt and pepper

LEEKS.

MUSTARD.

Trim and wash the leeks. Cook whole in a little boiling salted water for 10–12 minutes until tender but still holding their shape. Meanwhile, moisten the sausages with a little water and grill them, turning as needed, until evenly browned all over. Cut a few round slices of the drained leeks for garnishing; place the rest in an oven-to-table dish and arrange the sausages on top. Keep warm.

Melt the butter in a saucepan. Stir in the flour and cook, stirring, for 2 minutes. Gradually stir in the milk, then the cider. Simmer, still stirring, until the sauce thickens. Stir in the mustard and cheese. Season well.

Pour the sauce over the leeks and sausage. Bake at 350°F (180°C), Gas 4 for 5–8 minutes until the sauce is slightly gilded. Serve garnished with the reserved slices of leek.

'DEVILS' AND RELISHES

—◆◇◆—

'Devils'

Devilling is a British contribution to cookery, invented long ago as a way of masking the taste of tainted meat, poultry or game. By the eighteenth century, notorious for hard drinking, carousers had found a new use for it: they nibbled devilled snacks as a means of re-arousing a flagging thirst. By the staider Victorian age, however, 'devils' had become fashionable in another way. For those who could eat well, the breasts of home-shot game birds were a standard dinner entrée in autumn and winter, but to serve the legs was thought inelegant: a lady could hardly be expected to cut the meat off the solid bone, let alone pick it up and chew it. Victorian hostesses and housekeepers were, however, much too practical to discard the legs, and they were served up at breakfast, devilled and reheated, as a thrifty meat dish for the men of the family or the weekend shooting party.

We can still use 'devilling' to excellent purpose, to give extra flavour to modern poultry and snacks, and to make a change if we serve the same food often. If using it to 'ring the changes' on left-overs, apply the devilling mixture to the meat soon after cooking, while it is still warm if possible. Chill the meat as soon as it has cooled, and leave it for several hours before reheating it.

DEVILLING PEPPER

2 tsp table salt (2¹/2 tsp)	¹/4 tsp chilli powder (¹/2 tsp)
2 tsp ground black pepper (2¹/2 tsp)	cayenne pepper to taste

Mix all the ingredients. Use to rub over raw or cooked meat, especially round bone-ends and into any cuts before grilling them.

This mixture stores for 2–3 months in a sealed jar or pot.

DEVILLING MUSTARD FOR POULTRY OR GAME (*Makes about 1¹/2fl oz/35ml [3 tbsp]*)

2 tbsp anchovy essence (2¹/2 tbsp)	good pinch of grated nutmeg
good pinch of cayenne pepper	2 tsp dry English mustard (2¹/2 tsp)
¹/2 tsp curry powder (³/4 tsp)	2 tsp clear honey (2¹/2 tsp)

Mix all the ingredients until well blended. Score raw or cooked small pieces of poultry meat or joints with a knife-point. Spread with the mustard, and leave for at least 30 minutes. Then grill under medium heat, turning as needed, until raw meat is well cooked or cooked meat is heated right through.

Note: This devilling mixture is also good spread thinly on warm Bath Olivers or cocktail biscuits. It keeps perfectly in a covered jar in the refrigerator for a week or more, so make a double quantity to keep as a standby if you can.

DR KITCHINER'S DEVILLING MIXTURE, 1836 *(Makes about ¼pt/125ml [½cup + 2 tbsp])*

3 hard-boiled egg yolks	salad oil (as needed)
1½ tsp made English mustard (2 tsp)	finely chopped fresh tarragon or chervil (optional)
salt and pepper to taste	vinegar (optional)

Pound the egg yolks, mustard and seasoning to a paste. Stir in, gradually, enough oil to make a thin cream. Taste, and add the optional ingredients if you wish. Use for spreading on cooked meat or thin biscuits before grilling.

DEVILLING OR BARBECUE MARINADE *(Makes about 12fl oz/300ml [1½ cups])*

Ox or pigs' liver or kidneys become first-class tender meats if refrigerated in this marinade for 24–48 hours. A useful ploy if you cannot use them on the day you buy them!

3–4fl oz/75–100 ml tomato ketchup (⅓ cup)	¼ tsp anchovy essence (½ tsp)
2fl oz/50ml Worcester sauce (¼ cup)	4 tsp made English mustard (5 tsp)
¼pt/125ml salad oil (½ cup + 2 tbsp)	1 tsp clear honey (1¼ tsp)
	salt and ground black pepper to taste
	cayenne pepper to taste
	pinch of paprika (optional)

Mix all the ingredients until well blended. Cut raw or cooked meat into serving pieces, and score the flesh deeply with a knife-point. Place the marinade and meat in a stout plastic bag and seal securely. Leave in a shallow dish for several hours or overnight, turning the bag over two or three times. Dry the meat well before use.

Note: This marinade will keep for up to a week before use, if chilled.

DEVILLED DRUMSTICKS WITH CREAM SAUCE *(Serves 4)*

Here is an unusual way to turn leftover poultry or small game-bird legs into a delectable dish, fit for a party. You could use it, for instance, to cope with Christmas poultry leftovers for a Boxing Day buffet, using thick strips of turkey meat instead of drumsticks: or it may make a welcome change if you live in the country and get a surfeit of game birds during the shooting season.
Colour picture page 136

*4–6 pheasant, duck or chicken
  drumsticks (raw or cooked)
1 tbsp dry mustard (1¼ tbsp)
vinegar to taste
1½ tbsp Dundee marmalade
  (2 tbsp)
1½ tsp anchovy essence (2 tsp)
  or to taste*

*good pinch of cayenne pepper
salt*

FOR THE CREAM SAUCE:
*4 tsp butter (5 tsp)
½pt/250ml soured cream (1¼ cups)
salt and pepper
1–3 drops lemon juice*

Make several deep short slashes in the meat with a knife-point. Make the mustard, using a little vinegar instead of all water. Mix it with all the other devilling ingredients. Spread the mixture all over the meat, working it into the slashes if you can. Leave for at least 1 hour, longer if possible.

Lay the drumsticks side by side on a grill-pan rack. Grill, using high heat and turning as needed, until the pieces are crusty and well browned all over. Keep hot while making the sauce.

Melt the butter in a frying pan, over low heat. Stir in the cream, and boil gently for 2 minutes, stirring continuously. Season with salt, pepper and lemon juice. Place the drumsticks or turkey pieces in a serving dish with the bone-ends propped on the edge. Pour the bubbling sauce over them. Top the bone-ends with cutlet frills and serve at once.

A plain chicory or celery salad is all you need serve with the meat.

Relishes

A relish is usually a dab of spicy paste, sauce or chutney on the side of your plate, added to give your food extra flavour. Apart from the fact that, if you've cooked the dish wisely, using natural ingredients, it shouldn't *need* extra flavourings, most relishes don't so much add flavour as mask any that the dish already has. Some bought ones stun your palate and make it unfit to receive any food for hours afterwards. Luckily, you seldom eat enough to let them have the same effect on your stomach.

Having said that, there *are* relishes which are genuinely helpful to a dish, which complement its flavours or add a needed nutrient or texture. A curry is improved if one or two relishes are added to the small dishes of fresh fruit and herbs served with it. An Indonesian *rijsttafel* is a dish consisting entirely of curry-style relishes served with rice. When Italian pasta is served just with a thick tomato, garlic or walnut sauce, the whole interest of the dish (except to pasta addicts) is in the spicy relish. Barbecue relishes add a distinctive flavour to charcoal-grilled spare-ribs without destroying the flavour of the meat.

SPARE-RIB OF PORK.

You can make a relish from almost any savoury sauce or dip recipe by reducing the quantity of liquid; but strictly a relish should be a store-cupboard preserve, or made from one.

Here are one or two such relishes which support the flavours of foods you serve them with, rather than overwhelm them.

CHORON MUSTARD

4 tbsp Dijon mustard (5 tbsp)
4 tbsp concentrated tomato paste
  (5 tbsp)
1/2 tsp finely grated onion,
  optional (3/4 tsp)

lemon juice to taste
freshly ground black pepper

Mix together thoroughly the mustard and tomato paste. Add the grated onion. Season to taste with lemon juice and black pepper. Serve with hamburgers, pork chops, fried pork sausages or grilled liver and bacon.

MUSTARD AND CREAM RELISH

1/4pt/125ml soured cream
  (1/2 cup + 2 tbsp)
1 tbsp tarragon vinegar (1 1/4 tbsp)

2 tbsp finely chopped chives (2 1/2 tbsp)
1 tbsp French mustard (1 1/4 tbsp)
salt and pepper to taste

Mix all the ingredients thoroughly. Serve with boiled or grilled rabbit, grilled herrings or sausages.

[185]

YOGHURT RELISH

1/4 pt/125 ml natural yoghurt
   (1/2 cup + 2 tbsp)
2 oz/50 g mild Cheddar cheese,
   grated (1/3 cup)

1 egg yolk
1 tsp made English mustard (1 1/4 tsp)
salt and pepper

Mix all the ingredients in a small saucepan. Heat gently without boiling until the relish is thick and smooth, stirring continuously. Cool, or serve hot, on hot smoked cod or with any grilled fish or plainly simmered vegetables such as leeks.

EASTERN PEANUT RELISH

3 tbsp smooth peanut butter
   (4 tbsp)
1/2 tsp chilli powder (3/4 tsp)
1 tsp muscovado sugar (1 1/4 tsp)

1 tbsp lemon juice (1 1/4 tbsp)
   or to taste
salt (optional)

Mix the first three ingredients thoroughly, then gradually work in the lemon juice and any salt used, stirring thoroughly until incorporated. Serve with grilled kebabs, pickled fish or meat, or sharp-flavoured vegetables such as braised endive or celery.

PICKLES AND CHUTNEYS
—◆◆—

Colourful pickles and chutneys are a wonderful standby. You can dip into the pickle jar whenever you lack watercress or parsley for garnishing. Spicy fruit pickles, in particular, add zest to any meat dish, from game to sausage; by now we are used to eating various fruits with meat, not just redcurrant jelly and mint sauce.

Making pickles and chutneys is also an economical way to use windfalls or slightly blemished fruit, especially early types of apples which will not store well. You can make small quantities for 1–2 people just as easily as the usual bulk; only remember to pot the pickles in small jars, say the 1lb/450g size or smaller. If a jar contains more than you will eat in a day or two, you will probably have to re-seal it to prevent the vinegar evaporating, which is a nuisance.

Sweet pickles are quicker and easier to make than jam. They make a good alternative to jam too, if you like the slightly sharper, aromatic flavour.

[186]

Remember these three simple points when making any pickles:

If your vinegar mixture has to stand in the saucepan for more than a few moments, keep it covered, whether it is hot or cold.

Don't boil vinegar for a moment longer than you need to, but make sure any sugar in it has melted.

Use jars with secure vinegar-proof lids, ie not with metal or plastic inside. If you can, use jars which have held pickles before. If you haven't got any, the simple, cheap paraffin-wax method below is a good way of sealing jars, and you don't need lids at all; any uncracked jam-jars which are about the same thickness all over will do.

INDIA PICKLE.

To seal jars without lids

Buy a block of solid paraffin wax (hard paraffin) from a chemist. It is cheap, and keeps indefinitely. To use, chip off a chunk with a pointed knife, put the chunk in a saucepan and melt it very gently indeed. Make sure that any solids in the jar to be sealed are covered with cooled liquid and that there is at least ½in/1cm headspace above them; then pour the melted wax all over the liquid. Within a few minutes, it will be cloudy, then opaque. Label the jar with the type of pickle *and the date.*

Half-fill the saucepan with water and bring it to the boil, then let it stand until cold; any wax still left in the pan will be floating on top, and you can scoop it out and re-use it.

To take the seal off the pickles, run a sharp-pointed knife round the edge; then flip it off. If you pour a little water into a pan, and melt the wax seal in it, any pickle sticking to the wax will fall off. Let the wax cool, skim it off and store it for re-use.

Natural Pickles You can use honey or natural muscovado sugar for pickling if you wish, but they are expensive and tend to make the pickles look muddy. This is one of the few cases where it seems sensible to use white sugar; the beautifully coloured, distinct vegetables and fruit are more likely to be eaten, and their good food value used.

Spiced Vinegar for Pickles Unless you use whole spices a great deal, make spiced vinegar with bought pickling spice and perhaps a few extra whole cloves and black peppercorns. Making your own spice mixtures is interesting, but unless the spices are used up quickly they become musty in the jars and are fit for nothing. If you want to make your own mixture, try a 2in/5cm piece of cinnamon stick, 5–6 whole cloves, 1 tsp black peppercorns (1¼ tsp), 1 tsp whole allspice berries (1¼ tsp), ½ tsp mustard seed (¾ tsp), ½ tsp celery seed (¾ tsp), 2 fresh or 3 dried bay leaves, 2pt/1.1 litres (5 cups) white vinegar.

If you use bought ready-mixed pickling spice, add 4–5 tsp (5–6 tsp) to each 2pt/1.1 litres (5 cups) vinegar.

Put the vinegar and spices in a saucepan, cover and bring to the boil. Take the pan off the heat at once, and leave to stand, covered, for 3 hours. Strain into clean dry bottles, seal with vinegar-proof stoppers, label and store until wanted.

Pickles

APPLE PICKLE *(Fills four 1lb/450g jars)*

2lb/900g cooking apples or	*4 tbsp white sugar (5 tbsp), or to taste*
windfalls	*1oz/25g pickling spice or whole black*
1lb/450g mild onions	*peppercorns*
2oz/50g seeded raisins (¹/₃ cup)	*about ¹/₂pt/250ml white vinegar*
4 small hot red chillis	*(1¹/₄ cups)*
1 tbsp salt (1¹/₄ tbsp)	

Using low oven heat, warm four 1lb/450g jars and 1–2 small ones as spares. Peel and core the apples, and chop them into fair-sized pieces. Skin the onions and chop them finely. Mix both with the raisins. Stand the jars on a wooden surface, and pack in the mixture; bury 1 chilli in each jar. Leave a good ¾in/20mm headspace.

Put the salt, sugar, spice or peppercorns and vinegar in a saucepan, and bring to the boil. As soon as the sugar melts, pour the hot mixture into the jars, covering the fruit. Plunge a skewer into each jar, down to the bottom, two or three times, to let the vinegar filter right down. Leave the jars to cool, then seal and label as on page 187.

If you use ½lb/226g or other small jars, you may need extra vinegar. Just boil as much plain vinegar as you think you need, and use it to top up the jars.

[188]

ARTICHOKE PICKLE *(Fills three 1lb/450g jars)*

1pt/500ml cider vinegar (2¹/2 cups)
2 tbsp honey (2¹/2 tbsp)
¹/2 tbsp celery seed (³/4 tbsp)
¹/2 tbsp dill seed (³/4 tbsp)
¹/2oz/15g mustard seed (3¹/4 tsp)
¹/2 tbsp French mustard (³/4 tbsp)

³/4oz/20g coarse salt (2¹/2 tsp)
1 black peppercorn
1 small piece fresh ginger root
1lb/450g Jerusalem artichokes
3 young carrots

Bring the vinegar to the boil, remove from the heat, and add all the other ingredients except the ginger root, artichokes and carrots. Leave to cool.

While cooling, sterilise jars with vinegar-proof, airtight covers. Blanch the artichokes. Then slice the ginger root, artichokes and carrots thinly. Pack into the jars. Pour the cooled pickling liquid over them, to cover, then seal securely. Leave to mature for at least 1 month before use.

SWEET CARROT AND APPLE PICKLE *(Fills eight 1lb/450g jars)*

4lb/1.8kg cooking apples
1¹/2pt/850ml spiced or white
    vinegar (3³/4 cups)
1lb/450g medium carrots

2oz/50g seedless raisins (¹/3 cup)
¹/2–1 squeezed lemon, cut in shreds
2lb/900g white sugar

Without peeling, cut the apples into quarters or large pieces. Remove the cores and cut out any scabbed skin or bruises. Dip each piece at once in the vinegar, to prevent discolouring. Grate the carrots coarsely. Mix apples, carrot, raisins and lemon in a bowl.

Put vinegar and sugar in a large pan, and heat until the sugar dissolves. Add the fruit. Bring to the boil, and simmer (usually only for moments) until the apples are soft. Take out the fruit with a slotted spoon, and put at once into jars standing on a wooden surface; leave a good ³/4in/2cm headspace.

Boil the liquid (don't worry if some carrot shreds and raisins are left in it) down to 1¹/2pt/850ml (3³/4 cups) or slightly less; do not let it darken. Fill the jars with syrup, plunging a skewer deep into each jar several times, to let the syrup seep right down. Cover loosely. When cold, cover with vinegar-proof lids and label.

Pour any unused syrup into a square jar, cover and store it for next time round. Add enough plain vinegar to double its quantity.

SWEET BEETROOT PRESERVE *(Fills two 1lb/450g jars)*

Not quite a jam, nor yet a pickle. Excellent with ham or turkey, or as a side dish with curry.

2 small lemons
1pt/500ml sweet cider (2½ cups)
2½fl oz/65ml clear honey (¼ cup)
1lb/450g cooked beetroot, coarsely shredded

1 tsp ground ginger (1¼ tsp)
¼ tsp ground cinnamon (½ tsp)
2oz/50g skinned roasted hazelnuts, coarsely chopped (½ cup)

Slice the lemons thinly, discarding the ends. Cut the slices in half, and simmer with the cider for 15 minutes. Stir in the honey and beetroot, and continue simmering for another 20 minutes. Add the ginger, cinnamon and chopped nuts, and continue cooking for a further 15 minutes. Meanwhile, pour boiling water into 2 1lb/450g preserving or jam jars, and over the lids. Drain.

Spoon the preserve into the jars, and put on the lids loosely. When cold, tighten screw-bands or secure clip-on or lug-topped lids to seal. Label and store for up to 2 months.

SWEET PICKLED PEPPERS *(Fills one 1lb/450g jar)*

1 large (5oz/125g) or 2 small (3oz/ 75g) sweet red peppers
2 tsp dried sliced onions (2½ tsp)
8 tbsp white vinegar (about ½ cup)

4oz/100g white sugar (½ cup)
1in/2.5cm piece cinnamon stick
4 whole cloves

With a pointed knife, cut out the stems and remove the seeds of the peppers without breaking them. Prick the skins in several places with a poultry skewer. Put the peppers and onions in a heatproof bowl or jug.

Put the vinegar and sugar in a saucepan, and add the spices tied in a clean square of cloth. Bring the mixture to the boil, and as soon as the sugar has melted pour the liquid into the bowl or jug. Leave for 24 hours.

Re-boil the whole mixture for 5 minutes, then pack the vegetables into a hot jar standing on a wooden surface, and pour the vinegar syrup and onion over them, discarding the spices. Top up with extra vinegar if needed. Cool, seal, and label as on page 187.

Variation:
You can pickle 5oz/125g mung or lentil bean sprouts in exactly the same way, but leave them to soak for only 4–6 hours.

Chutneys
Like fruit pickles, chutneys are excellent for using up less than perfect fruit; if you include dried fruit, you have all the goodness of that too, and need less sugar.

ALL-SORTS CHUTNEY

3–4lb/1.3–1.8kg mixed sharp-flavoured fruit plus tomato and marrow
8oz–1lb/200–450g onions, to taste
1–1¹/₂ tsp ground spices (see method) (1¹/₄–1³/₄ tsp)

¹/₄ tsp salt (¹/₂ tsp)
8oz/200g mixed dried fruit (1¹/₃ cups)
1pt/500ml white or red vinegar (2¹/₂ cups)
8–14oz/200–375g brown sugar, as fruit requires

Prepare the fruit: peel, core and slice apples, skin tomatoes, peel and de-seed marrow, stone plums etc. Skin and chop the onions and simmer in a little water until tender. Add the prepared fruit, then the spices, salt, dried fruit and vinegar. Choose spices which suit the flavour of the fruit: cinnamon or nutmeg, coriander, cardomum, mixed spice, allspice, clove are all good with most fruits. Simmer until well blended, then add the sugar and stir until dissolved. Place jars to heat in the oven.

Raise the heat and boil the chutney, stirring occasionally, until the mixture is firm with no free liquid. Put into the heated jars, cover lightly and allow to cool. Seal tightly when quite cold, and store until required.

GOOSEBERRY MINT *(Makes ³/₄pt/375ml [scant 2 cups])*

1¹/₂lb/700g gooseberries
2 large bunches mint
7¹/₂fl oz/185ml wine or cider vinegar (scant 1 cup)

1lb/450g white sugar (3¹/₂ cups)

Top and tail the gooseberries, and remove any wilted or discoloured leaves from the mint. Rinse both briefly. Put the gooseberries and 1 bunch of mint in a preserving pan with the vinegar, and simmer until the berry skins are tender but not broken. Remove the mint. Add the sugar, and continue simmering until it has dissolved.

Leave on the side of the stove, while you bruise the remaining mint and chop the bruised leaves finely. Add them to the pan, bring to the boil, and boil until the preserve is as thick as chutney. Put into heated jars, cover lightly and allow to cool. Seal tightly when quite cold.

[191]

11

GOOD VALUE TREATS

———◆◇◆———

Nearly everyone likes a sweet treat sometimes. Sweets made with refined sugar and flavouring only supply quickly used calories with an energy slump afterwards, at serious risk to both one's teeth and figure. If you make your own sweets, however, you can blend the sweetening with real butter and with nuts or bran, or, better still, use dried fruits; then they'll have wholesome nutritive value as well as all the sweetness you could wish.

DATE ROLLS *(Makes about 20)*
Dried fruit and seeds are nourishing as well as good to taste. Children will enjoy making the rolls — and getting *very* sticky.

8oz/200g block stoneless cooking
dates (1 cup)
1oz/25g seedless raisins
(scant 1/4 cup)

2oz/50g butter, softened (1/4 cup)
2fl oz/50ml honey (1/4 cup)
2 tbsp beaten egg (21/2 tbsp)
4oz/100g sunflower seeds (2/3 cup)

Chop the dates and raisins finely. Mix them in a saucepan with the butter, honey and egg. Stirring briskly, heat gently until the butter melts, and the mixture bubbles. Still stirring, cook for 1 minute or until the mixture leaves the bottom of the pan clean. Remove from the heat at once. Cool. While cooling, chop the seeds finely in a food processor or blender, and mix them in.

Chill the mixture. When firm, form into rolls, the same shape as whole dates. Refrigerate until needed.

[192]

CHOCOLATE ALMOND CRUNCH *(Makes 1 1/2 lb/700g pieces)*

4oz/100g split almonds (1 cup)
1 tbsp hot water (1 1/4 tbsp)
1 tbsp instant coffee powder
   (1 1/4 tbsp)

8oz/200g caster sugar (1 cup)
6oz/150g unsalted butter (3/4 cup)
4oz/100g plain chocolate

Spread the almonds on a baking sheet. Grill for 1–2 minutes, turning if needed, until golden. Leave to cool.

Grease an 11in x 7in/275mm x 175mm baking tin. Mix the water, coffee powder, sugar and butter in a saucepan, and heat gently, with a thermometer in the pan, stirring continuously, until the sugar dissolves. Boil until the mixture reaches 280°F (140°C), when a little dropped into cold water will separate into hard threads. Remove from the heat and stir in 2oz/50g of the almonds. Spread evenly in the baking tin, and leave to cool.

Melt the chocolate in a bowl over hot water. Spread it on the toffee, and sprinkle with the remaining almonds. Leave until the chocolate has set, then break into pieces.

COFFEE TRUFFLES *(Makes about 16)*

1 tbsp instant coffee powder
   (1 1/4 tbsp)
3 tbsp sifted cocoa (4 tbsp)
2 tbsp honey (2 1/2 tbsp)
1oz/25g dried skimmed milk
   (1/4 cup)

1 tbsp unsalted butter, softened
   (1 1/4 tbsp)
1/2 tsp Tia Maria or orange juice
   (3/4 tsp)
5 tsp golden granulated sugar (8 tsp)
1 tsp ground cinnamon (1 1/4 tsp)

Mix the coffee powder, cocoa and honey in a small saucepan. Stir over low heat for 3 minutes or until blended and syrupy. Remove from heat and work in the milk powder, butter, flavouring and 2 tsp (2 1/2 tsp) sugar. Refrigerate until firm. Roll into small balls.

Mix the remaining sugar and the cinnamon, and roll the truffles in the mixture, to coat. Refrigerate until needed.

COUNTRY WALNUT TOFFEE *(Makes about 45 squares)*

4oz/100g unsalted butter (1/2 cup)
8oz/200g light muscovado sugar
   (1 cup)

8oz/200g golden syrup (1 1/4 cups light
   molasses)
4oz/100g walnut pieces

Grease an 11in x 7in/275mm x 175mm baking tin. Melt the butter in a thick saucepan. Stir in the sugar and syrup, and heat gently with a thermometer in the pan until the sugar dissolves. Bring to the boil, and cook until the thermometer registers 280°F (140°C), when a little dropped into cold water will separate into hard but not brittle threads.

Meanwhile, chop the walnuts. Remove the toffee from the heat, and stir in the nuts. Pour into the tin. Leave until nearly set, then mark in squares. Break when cold.

INSTANT FUDGE SQUARES *(Makes 36 pieces)*
Quick to make, easy and always popular.

6oz/150g sweetened bran breakfast cereal (3 cups)
2 tbsp honey (2½ tbsp)
4oz/100g unsalted butter (½ cup)
2oz/50g light muscovado sugar (¼ cup)

2oz/50g unsweetened cocoa powder (½ cup)
¼ tsp vanilla essence (½ tsp)

Grease a 7in/175mm shallow tin. Crush the bran cereal to fine even crumbs.

Melt the honey, butter and sugar over low heat, sift in the cocoa, and stir for 2 minutes until fully blended and syrupy. Off the heat, work in the bran cereal crumbs and essence. Press evenly into the tin. Blot off any excess fat, and mark into 36 squares.

Chill for 24 hours. Cut or break into squares, and serve in sweet cases.

NUT CRUNCH BARS *(Makes about 20)*

2 egg whites
4 tbsp warmed clear honey (5 tbsp)
4oz/100g coarsely ground almonds
  or mixed nuts (1 cup)

4 Weetabix, crushed to crumbs
pinch of salt

Whisk the egg whites stiffly in a large bowl. Still whisking, gradually add the honey, and whisk until stiff and glossy. Fold in the nuts, salt and Weetabix crumbs. Grease an 11in x 7in/275mm x 175mm shallow baking tin. Spread the meringue mixture in an even layer over its base. Bake at 325°F (160°C), Gas 3 for 25–30 minutes until firm and lightly browned. Cool in the tin, then cut into bars.

APRICOT MUSCOVADOS *(Makes 24–26)*

6oz/150g dried apricots (1 cup)
2oz/50g unsalted butter (¼ cup)
2fl oz/50ml water (¼ cup)
8oz/200g light muscovado sugar
  (1 cup)

1 tsp lemon juice (1¼ tsp)
2fl oz/50ml single cream (¼ cup light
  cream)
extra light muscovado sugar as needed
desiccated coconut (optional)

Wash and dry the apricots. Chop very finely. Melt the butter in a non-stick saucepan, and add water, sugar and lemon juice. With a thermometer in the pan, bring the mixture to the boil, and heat to 240°F (115°C) or until a little mixture dropped into cold water forms a soft ball. Lift off the heat and stir in the cream. Return to the heat and stir ceaselessly until mixture reaches 250°F (120°C) or forms a hard ball when dropped in cold water. Remove from the heat, and stir in the apricots, mixing thoroughly. Leave to cool.

When cold, roll into 1in/2.5cm balls; roll in extra sugar and coconut if you wish, and put in sweet cases. Keep refrigerated until eaten (this will not be for long).

[195]

BOOKS TO READ

When I was looking for old, thrifty recipes and ideas which might interest us today, I turned time and time again to five past authors both for their practical inventiveness and for reading pleasure. The books of four of them have been published in facsimile, so should be available from any Public Library if you wish to refer to them.

> Acton, Eliza *Modern Cookery for Private Families* (1845; Elek Books, 1966)
> Beeton, Isabella (ed) *Beeton's Book of Household Management* (1861; Jonathan Cape, 1968)
> Glasse, Hannah *The Art of Cookery Made Plain and Easy* (1747; S. R. Publishers, 1971)
> Raffald, Elizabeth *The Experienced English Housekeeper* (1769; E & W Books, 1970)

The fifth book, *The Compleat Housewife or Accomplish'd Gentlewoman's Companion* by E. Smith has not been republished, nor have most of the later Victorian cookery books in which convenience foods appear as the new 'in' thing, but one can still find quite a number of these by rummaging on bookstalls and in libraries.

Useful modern books which deal with particular aspects of natural and wholefood cookery and preserving are:

> Allison, Sonia *Book of Preserving* (David & Charles, 1979)
> Black, Maggie and Howard, Pat *Eating Naturally* (Faber, 1980)
> David, Elizabeth *Salt, Spices and Aromatics in the English Kitchen* (Penguin, 1970)
> Dixon, Pamela *Pulse Cookery* (Thoisens, 1980)
> Elliot, Rose *Not Just a Load of Old Lentils* (Fontana, 1972)
> Loewenfeld, Claire and Back, Philippa *The Complete Book of Herbs and Spices* (David & Charles, 1978)
> Martin, Faye *Naturally Delicious Desserts* (Rodale Press, 1980)
> Reekie, Jennie *Everything Raw* (Penguin, 1978)
> Wadey, Rosemary *Baking Country Breads and Pastries* (David & Charles, 1980)

ACKNOWLEDGEMENTS

———◆◇◆———

The author and publisher owe a special debt of thanks to the following for specially taken pictures: Colman's Mustard, Jif Lemon Juice, Gale's Honey Ltd. Sincere thanks are also due to the following for pictures and recipes: Butter Information Council, Van den Bergh's and Jurgens Ltd, Potato Marketing Board, British Bacon Bureau, British Sausage Bureau, CPC (United Kingdom) Ltd, Sarson's Vinegars Ltd, Dufrais Ltd, Mushroom Growers' Association, Allinson's Ltd, New Zealand Lamb Information Bureau, British Chicken, Swiss Cheese Information Service, Wheelbarrow Unsalted Butter, Edward Billington and Sons Ltd, Weetabix Ltd, Porter's Restaurant, Christopher Snook, British Farm Produce Council, British Duck Advisory Bureau, Batchelors Ltd and Coates Gaymer Ciders.

Ward Lock Ltd generously allowed the use of black and white illustrations from the 1888 edition of Mrs Beeton's *Cookery and Household Management*.

The book would not have seen the light of day without the patient testing and kindly, efficient typing and checking done by Marcelle Letacq and Pauline Wilson.

Finally, it would certainly not have been achieved without the ideas and creative help provided by Mesdames E. Smith, Elizabeth Raffald, Hannah Glasse, Eliza Acton, Beeton and other eighteenth and nineteenth-century cooks.

INDEX

All-sorts chutney, 191
Almond butter, Mrs Smith's, 74
American coffee cakes, 79
American muffins, 91
Anchovy butter, 74
Apple: and blackberry jam, 109; and carrot pickle, 189; and celery salad, 124; bread, Old English, 90; Brown Betty, 97; butter, 110; cake, Farmhouse bran, 164; dumplings, sausage and, 180; Lamb cakes with, 23; pickle, 188; pudding, 167; purée, 163; purée with chutney, 169; *see also* Cidered pigeons, 56
Apricot muscovados, 195
Artichoke pickle, 189
Aubergine (eggplant): rounds, 129; spread or dip, 114

Bacon: and apple pie, 165; and cheese well, 66; collar of, Honey-glazed, 180; Liver and, 30; English potted, 105; uses of, 176; *see also* Choucroute garni, 178; Fish chowder, 35; Harlequin salad, 124; Meat-filled cannelloni, 28; Slipper pudding, 179;
Baked: carrot casserole, 138; cheese gnocchi, 68; oatmeal bannock, 90; ploughman's brunch, 67
Baking-powder bread, plain, 89
Banded fish loaf, 36
Barbecue marinade, 183
Barley scones, 92
Barnstaple buns, 92
Basil vinegar, 147
Beef as you like it, 19
Beef Collops (1860), 21
Beetroot in Jellied crown salad, 126
Beetroot preserve, sweet, 190
Beurre noir, 151
Biscuits, devilled, 183
Blackberry and apple jam, 109
Boeuf à la mode, 19
Bottled oranges, 172

Bread: baking powder, Plain, 89; Herb, 84; Mushroom, 86; Old English apple, 90; Potato, 85; stale, uses of, 81, 95–9; to store, 81; Wholemeal, 82; Wholemeal egg, 83
Breads, yeast, 82–8
Breadcrumbs: Buttered, 97; pastry flan case, 96; pastry mix, 96; types to use, 10
Brioche rolls, wholemeal, 83
Broccoli salad, 122
Brown: Betty, 97; onion sauce, 23; sauce, English, 23
Buns:
Barnstaple, 92; Fresh orange, 93; Savoury cornmeal, 91; Spiced yeast, 88; stale, uses of, 79
Butter icing, basic, 76
Butters: herb, 149–151; sweet and savoury, 74–6
Buttercream, basic, 77

Cabbage and seed salad, 122
Cakes: butter icing for, 76; buttercream for, 77; Farmhouse bran apple cake, 164; Mrs Beeton's school, 174; Prune spice, 173; Rhubarb, 158; Victorian coconut gingerbread, 94; Wholemeal gingerbread, 93
Canapé butter, 151
Canned foods, 10, 11, 12, 119, 132–4
Carrot: and apple pickle, sweet, 189; casserole, Baked, 138
Carrots, glazed, 128
Casseroles: Baked carrot, 138; beans and tomatoes, 133; Cidered chicken, 45; Gloucester, Veal and lemon, 26; *see also* mandarin pigeons, 58; Rabbit layers, 61
Cauliflower: 'cake', creamy, 70; steamed, 129
Celeriac salad, 121
Celery and apple salad, 124
Champ, Parsley, 140
Champ, Spring onion, 141

Cheese: and tomato spread, 113; bacon and, well, 66; baked, gnocchi, 68; pots, 166; uses of, 63–4
see also
Aubergine rounds, 129; Aubergine spread, 114; Bacon and apple pie, 165; Baked Ploughman's Brunch, 67; Courgette leaves, 128; Derbyshire butter, 74; Gloucestershire casserole, 68; Rarebits, 69; Sausage, leek and cider bake, 181; Severn crumble, 38
Chicken: and mushroom pâté; baskets, 46; Cidered, casserole, 45; Country, 48; crisps, 45; drumsticks, with cream sauce, 184; fat, to 'make', 42; giblet soup, 50; in jelly (Mrs Glasse's fowl), 43; Lemon-baked, with crisps, 45; liver pâté, 50; salad wheel, 47
see also Pupton of pigeons, 59
Chive butter, 150
Chocolate almond crunch, 193
Choron mustard, 185
Choucroute garni, 178
Chutney, 191; All-sorts, 191; apple purée with, 182
Cidered chicken casserole, 44
Cidered pigeons, 56
Cod cutlets, crusted, 35
Coffee truffles, 193
Collared breast of lamb, 25
Country chicken and mushroom pâté, 48
Country walnut toffee, 193
Courgette leaves, 128
Creamy cauliflower 'cake', 70
Crusted cod cutlets, 35

Date rolls, 192
Derbyshire butter, 74
Desserts: Apple pudding, 167; applecake, Farmhouse bran, 164; Brown Betty, 97; Evesham crumble, 162; Farmhouse plum pudding, 171; Guard's pudding, 98; Pear and coconut crumble,

[198]

168; Poor knights of Windsor, 99; Raspberry pot pie, 160; Somerset plum syllabub, 162; Sparkling peach condé, 159; Spinach pudding, 72; Walnut and sultana pudding, 97
Devilled drumsticks with cream sauce, 184
Devilling
  marinade, 183
  mixture, Dr Kitchiner's, 183
  mustard, 182
  pepper, 182
'Devils', 182–4
Dips: Aubergine, 114; Ham and spring onion, 114; Herb and egg, 155
Dripping: as topping, 101; cakes, 101; in Barnstaple buns, 92; in Mrs Beeton's school cake, 174; in oatmeal bannock, 90; in wholemeal gingerbread, 93; to render/clarify, 102; toast, 101
Dumplings, sausage and apple, 180

Eastern peanut relish, 186
Egg: balls, 34; bread, wholemeal, 83; herb and, dip, 155 see also Creamy cauliflower 'cake', 70; Ploughman's Omelette, 97; Spinach Pudding, 72; Turnip soufflé, 71
Eggplant see Aubergine, 129
Eggs, use of, 54–5
English brown sauce, 23
Evesham crumble, 162

Faggots, 30
Fairy butter, Mrs Beeton's, 75
Farmhouse bran applecake, 165
Farmhouse plum pudding, 171
Fats, to clarify, 42, 102
Fig filler, 169
Fish and 'chips' casserole, 39
Fish:
  chowder, 35; dishes, 32–9; see also Anchovy butter, 74; Potted smoked haddock, 106
Fowl in Jelly, Mrs Glasse's, 43
French beans soubise, 134
Fresh orange buns, 93
Fresh raspberry sauce, 160
Fresh soft fruit syrups, 161
Fruit: canned, uses of, 11; chutneys, 191; dried in sweets, 192, 195; juices as sweeteners, 14; pickles, 186, 188–90; purées, 157; shortcake, 81; spreads, 107–9; storage of, 156–7; syrups,

161; using in autumn and winter, 165–74; using in summer, 158–64
Fudge squares, Instant, 194

Garlic butter, 150; oil, 148
Georgian poultry livers, 49
Gigot chops with red cabbage, 22
Gingerbread, Victorian coconut, 194; wholemeal, 93
Glazed carrots, 138
Gloucester casserole, 68
Gooseberry mint, 191
Guard sauce, 75
Guard's pudding, 98

Ham and spring onion dip, 114
Harlequin salad, 124
Herb:
  and egg dip, 155; and pork meat pâté, 153; breads, 84; butter, 150; butters, 149–51; oils, 148–9; vinegars, 144–7
Herbs, to dry, 143–4; uses of (recipes), 152–55
Honey, use of, 13
Honey-glazed collar of bacon, 180
Home-made tomato sauce, 25

Imperial Russian salad, 134
Instant fudge squares, 194

Jellied crown salad, 126
Junction salad, 125

Lamb turnovers with beans, 24
Leek scramble, 130
Lemon-baked chicken with crisps, 45
Lemon curd, 112
Liver and bacon, 30
Liver pâté, 105
Liver pâté, chicken, 50

Mandarin pigeons, 58
Maitre d'hotel butter, 150
Marinades: devilling, for meat, 183; for celeriac, 121; for Fish kebabs, 32; for kidneys, 31; in lemon juice, 121; uses of, 17
Marinated fish kebabs, 32
Marinated kidneys, 31
Marron, Mock, 113
Marrow with hot salad stuffing, 166
Meat: 19–31; devilled, 182–4; filled cannelloni, 28; loaf, mixed, 29; see also Bacon and apple pie, 165; Bacon and cheese well, 66; Baked

ploughman's brunch, 67; Derbyshire butter, 74; Fish chowder, 35; Fish and 'chip' casserole, 39; Gloucester casserole, 68; Harlequin salad, 124; Marrow with hot salad stuffing, 166; Quick-simmered medley, 131
Melba sauce, 160
Melon and cucumber, Minted, 152
Mincemeat, 172
Mint butter, 150
Mint vinegar, 146
Minted melon and cucumber, 152
Mock marron, 113
Montpelier butter, 150
Mrs Beeton's fairy butter, 75
Mrs Beeton's school cake, 174
Mrs Glasse's fowl in jelly, 43
Mrs Smith's almond butter, 74
Mushrooms: and watercress salad, 123; bread, 86; Country chicken and, pâté, 48
Mushrooms, Potted, 106
Mushrooms, Sofa, 137
Mustard and cream relish, 185

Nut crunch bars, 195

Oatmeal bannock, Baked, 90; drop scones, 87
Oils: herb, 149; types to use, 11
Old English apple bread, 90
Omelette, Ploughman's, 97
Onion and pepper salad, sweet, 125
Onion sauce, Brown, 23
Oranges, Bottled, 172

Parcelled hearts, 29
Parsley champ, 140
Parsnip purée, 141
Pastry: for Bacon and apple pie, 165; for St George's pie, 170; for Sausage and apple dumplings, 180; for Slipper pudding, 179; buttercrust, 167; flan case, breadcrumb, 96; mix, breadcrumb, 96; pressed, 27
Pâté: Chicken liver, 50; Country chicken and mushroom, 48; Herb and pork meat, 153; Liver, 105; see also Banded fish loaf, 36; Mixed meat loaf, 29; Springtime loaf, 139
Pâtés, 103–6; fats for, 101
Peanut relish, Eastern, 186
Pear and coconut crumble, 168
Pepper and onion salad, sweet, 125

Pickled peppers, Sweet, 190
Pickles, 186–190
Pigeons: Cidered, 56; Mandarin, 58; Roast stuffed, 57
Ploughman's brunch, baked, 67
Ploughman's omelette, 97
Plum: 'cheese', Spiced, 111; pudding, Farmhouse, 171; syllabub, Somerset, 167
Pork, English potted, 105
Potted foods, 103–6; bacon, 105; beef, 104; mushrooms, 106; pork, 105; smoked haddock, 106
Poultry dishes, 43–62
Preserves: apple butter, 110; apple purée, 163; Blackberry and apple jam, carrot and apple pickle, 189; Gooseberry mint, 191; Lemon curd, 112; Mock marron, 112; peppers, Pickled, 190; Seville orange marmalade, 110; Spiced rhubarb, 108; Sweet, beetroot 190
Prune spice cake, 173
Pupton of pigeons or turkey, 59

Quick apple purée, 163
Quick-simmered medley, 131

Rabbit: Curried, 61; layers, 61; Stifado, 62; see also Derbyshire butter, 74; Pupton of pigeons, 59; Quicksimmered medley, 131
Rarebits, cheese, 69
Raspberry pot pie, 160
Raspberry sauce, fresh, 160
Ratatouille, 139
Relishes, 182, 185–6
Rhubarb cake, 158
Rhubarb jam, spiced, 108
Roast stuffed pigeons, 57
Rose vinegar, 147
Rosemary oil, 148

St George's pie, 170
Salad dressings: Chapon, 154; for Celeriac salad, 121; for Harlequin salad, 124; for Mushroom and water-

cress salad, 123; Tarragon mayonnaise, 155; see also Garlic oil, 149; Mint vinegar, 146; Rosemary oil, 148
Salad sandwich spread, 114
Salad-stuffed rolls, 154
Salads, 120–6; Celeriac, 121; Chicken wheel, 47; Imperial Russian, 134; Jellied crown, 126;Junction, 125; Minted melon and cucumber, 152; stir-fry, Sweet-sour (hot), 130; stuffed rolls, 154; stuffing, Marrow with (hot), 166; winter, 121
Sauces: Beurre noir, 150; Brown onion, 23; Devilled drumsticks with cream, 184; Curry for rabbit, 61; Custard with lemon, 167; English brown, 23; for Meat-filled cannelloni, 28; for Roast stuffed pigeons, 57; Fresh raspberry, 160; Guard, 75; Home-made tomato, 25; quick apple, 163; Strawberry jam, 98
Sausage (and sausage meat); and apple dumplings, 180; leek and cider bake, 181; see also Country chicken and mushroom pâté, 48; Fish and 'chip' casserole, 39
Sausages, description and use of, 176–7
Savoury cornmeal buns, 91
Scones: Baked oatmeal (bannock), 90; barley, 92; oatmeal drop, 87; uses of 79, 81
Sesame chicken, 46
Severn crumble, 38
Seville orange marmalade, 110
Shallot butter, 150
Sheep's hearts, Parcelled, 29
'Short' cooking, 127–31
Slipper pudding, 179
Sofa mushrooms, 137
Somerset plum syllabub, 162
Soups: Chicken or turkey giblet, 50; Fish chowder, 35; Tomato and thyme, 152; see also Egg balls as garnish for, 72
Sparkling peach condé, 159

Spinach pudding, 72
Spreads and fillings, 74–7, 100–14, 149–51
Spring onion champ, 141
Springtime loaf, 139
Steamed cauliflower, 129
Stir-frying, 127
Stuffings: fig, 169; for Cannelloni, 28; for Parcelled hearts, 29; for Pomander duck, 55; for Roast pigeons, 57; Hot salad in marrow, 166; Mincemeat, 172; salad for rolls, 152
Sweet-sour salad stir-fry, 130

Tarragon: butter, 150; mayonnaise, 155; vinegar, 147
Tomato: and cheese spread, 113; and thyme soup, 152; sauce, Home-made 25
Turnip soufflé, 71
Turkey, 43; giblet soup, 50; in Georgian poultry livers, 49; Pupton of, 59; see also Sesame chicken, 46

Veal and lemon casserole, 26
Vegetable dishes (hot), 127–41 see also Creamy cauliflower 'cake', 70; Spinach pudding (sweet), 72; Turnip soufflé, 71
Vegetables, how to handle, 115–19
Victorian coconut gingerbread, 94
Victorian stewed fish, 37

Walnut and sultana pudding, 97
Walnut toffee, Country, 193
Watercress and mushroom salad, 123
Watercress butter, 150
Wholemeal: bread, 82; brioche rolls, 83; egg bread, 83; gingerbread, 93; rolls, 82
Wholemeal and low-extraction flours, 9, 12, 79
Winter casserole, 20

Yeast buns, spiced, 88
Yoghurt relish, 186